Flapper Era Fashions
From the Roaring '20s

Tina Skinner
&
Lindy McCord

Schiffer Publishing Ltd ®

4880 Lower Valley Road, Atglen, PA 19310 USA

Managing Editor - Tina Skinner

Editors - Lindy McCord and Ginny Parfitt

Designer - John Cheek

Cover Designer - Bruce Waters

Library of Congress Cataloging-in-Publication Data:

Skinner,Tina.
 Flapper era fashions from the Roaring 20s / by Tina Skinner & Lindy McCord.
    p. cm.
  ISBN 0-7643-2075-0 (pbk.)
1. Clothing and dress—History—20th century. 2. Women's clothing—History—20th century. 3. Nineteen twenties. I. McCord, Lindy. II. Title.
GT596.S55 2004
391'.2'0904—dc22
                              2004011810

Designed by John P. Cheek
Cover design by Bruce Waters
Type set in Americana XBd BT/Zurich BT

ISBN: 0-7643-2075-0
Printed in China

Published by Schiffer Publishing Ltd.
4880 Lower Valley Road
Atglen, PA 19310
Phone: (610) 593-1777; Fax: (610) 593-2002
E-mail: Info@schifferbooks.com

For the largest selection of fine reference books on this and related subjects, please visit our web site at **www.schifferbooks.com**
We are always looking for people to write books on new and related subjects. If you have an idea for a book please contact us at the above address.

This book may be purchased from the publisher.
Include $3.95 for shipping.
Please try your bookstore first.
You may write for a free catalog.

In Europe, Schiffer books are distributed by
Bushwood Books
6 Marksbury Ave.
Kew Gardens
Surrey TW9 4JF England
Phone: 44 (0) 20 8392-8585; Fax: 44 (0) 20 8392-9876
E-mail: info@bushwoodbooks.co.uk
Free postage in the U.K., Europe; air mail at cost.

Contents

Introduction

When we think of the early twentieth century, almost everyone associates the Roaring '20s with a tumultuous time of organized crime, alcohol rebellion and prohibition, and sexy dresses with fringe and flair. Calvin Coolidge was guiding post World War I America through a time of reconstruction and revolution. Hollywood graduated from silent pictures to "talkies." Women gained stature and respect, and the passing of the 19th Amendment gave them the right to vote. The country was making a desperate effort to improve and "grow up," as were men's and women's fashions.

With the arrival of the Mid 1920s, everyday Americans were enjoying Haute Couture, as mass production made high fashions accessible to everyone. This era marked the beginning of the prêt-a-porte (ready to wear) movement in America. With women gaining independence in the workplace and stature in society, they didn't want to waste time on lengthy fittings.

Due to the nationwide exploitation of mass media, fads could spring up overnight and die just as quickly. Skirt lengths fluctuated, but found a home just above the knee by 1926; this is the shortest American women would see their hemlines throughout the 1920s. Haircuts were short. The "bob" swept through hairdressing salons worldwide, attributed to fashionable parisians.

Women wore mannish styles too – no bosom, no waistline, and hair nearly hidden under a cloche hat. The most desirable silhouette was that of an adolescent girl – skinny, with narrow boyish hips and a flat chest with no womanly curves. This came to be known as the Flapper Age. The name denoted a young, trendy woman who wore the latest fashions, donned make-up, and was a wage-earner with a job. She would go on dates without a chaperone, and sought entertainment in dark, smoky lounges, dancing until the sun came up. She was exerting her freedom and her independence and her attire reflected this change in attitude.

This decade launched the modern cosmetics industry. Flappers wore powder, lipstick, rouge, eyebrow pencil, eye shadow, and had colored nails. The different looks of the period were practically dictated by Coco Chanel. She introduced the simple look of a two-piece suit, cardigan jacket, jersey blouse, and the distinctive look of a single string of pearls. Although these fashions were plain and uncomplicated, women embraced them and added their own style and flavor.

Lingerie was worn explicitly for support, and if anything, was utilized to conceal. Modern day corsets were abandoned in favor of the bust bodice or brassiere, essential under an evening dress to give a flatter, more slenderized appearance. Bras were simple and minimizing, avoiding any suggestive form.

Accessories started to play a larger role in fashion as the decade continued. Now, with shorter dresses, shoes were clearly visible and needed to be selected with more care. Many heels were over two inches high, and had attractive straps and latticework, fastening with unique buttons and closures. Strapped shoes, often known as Mary Janes were the most popular style of the 1920s. T-bar shoes or others with buckles and bows made interesting fashion statements, and could be trimmed with lace, sequins, or diamanté.

Men's fashions were straightforward – attractive single- or double-breasted suits for business attire, with exaggerated shoulders and emphasizing narrow hips. Sturdy denim and twill overalls and coveralls were standard for blue collar workers. Sporting attire became more popular, with an emphasis on golf and polo shirts, knickers, and other attire for manly outdoor activities. Children often were dressed to honor recent war heroes. Their everyday attire mimicked that of their parents, but with bright, lively colors to accentuate their youthful fervor.

The following images, from the Bellas Hess & Co. Spring and Summer 1925 catalog, and the Charles Williams Stores, Inc. Spring Summer 1927 catalog, offer an historic overview of everyday fashions in America. The original catalog language has been abridged in the image captions.

Men, women, and children were stepping out in style throughout the 1920s!

Sitting pretty in a luscious silk dress.

Women's Fashions

Day Wear

Dressy or casual, New York women sport
the highest fashion, and so should you!

All silk flat crepe with shirred ruffles and a soft cameo-like buckle on the side, in Cedarwood and rose sleeve, or Gracklehead blue and French blue sleeve. Silk and cotton printed crepe, string belt, novelty ball buttons, Navy blue or rose. Button-front crepe rayon dress, tan, Claret red, Gracklehead blue.

All wool crepe with neatly tailored long sleeves, all silk foulard with georgette collar, all wool flannel or jersey cotton frocks. Ideal for sport and play. Navy blue, brown, Gracklehead blue, and Rosewood.

A new tiered frock, in all silk flat crepe. Georgette crepe at the neck and waistline, metallic ribbon adds to its distinctiveness and richness. Black and Logwood, a stunning afternoon frock, plain color Crepe de Chine with an embroidered net jabot at the neck. Navy and tan.

Colorful dresses in the latest styles! Lightweight and comfortable for summer. All silk georgette crepe, flat crepe, flowered Crepe de Chine, rayon crepe. These types of dresses young women can wear to school, for business, to parties, or even for street wear.

New and smart style features in women's dresses… scalloped front all silk flat crepe with detachable vestee and double collar, Navy blue and crystal gray. Coat dress of flowered rayon in artificial silk and cotton with lines that are simple, chic, and becoming. Gracklehead blue, rose, and tan. Another smart looking rayon crepe frock in semi-sport type with Peter Pan collar and smart Windsor bow tie at neck. Gracklehead blue, rosewood, and tan.

Radium tub silk frock with sharp V-design, pleated skirt. Copenhagen blue and tan. A Flock Dot Voile frock should be in every woman's wardrobe, with smart ruffles on side and tuxedo collar of rich ecru net, Navy, rose, and orchid. High luster rayon frock with groups of tucks extending the length, giving a slender appearance. Copenhagen blue, tan, and lavender.

All silk flat crepe frock, long blouse effect with flounce and group of pleats in front. Navy, Cedarwood, figured Voile with a cascading jabot and girdle, becoming buckle with crushed belt in front. Copenhagen blue, tan, and navy. Richly embroidered frock of fine Voile, puffed bishop sleeves and finely knife pleated flounce. Copenhagen blue, Peach, and Reseda Green.

Printed voile dress with lace vestee, scalloped side panels and collar, crushed girdle, and novelty buckle in front. All silk charmeuse with contrasting appliqués and allover embroidery design. Printed rayon Tussah with pockets and collar trimmed with rich looking lace and lace vestee. Coat frock of jacquard rayon with wide tuxedo front, narrow belt of self material with novelty buckle.

Slenderizing styles, embroidered voile, all silk flat crepe, silk and cotton print, or striped mohair afternoon dresses for full figures. Navy, gray, black, logwood, or Copenhagen blue.

Chic coat, wool-mixed plaid effectively trimmed with contrasting colors, deep patch pockets with novelty buttons, gray or tan mixture. Smart poke hat fashioned of woven straw body and beautifully trimmed with mixed floral and fruit wreath, close fitting and becoming for spring and summer. All silk crepe de Chine frock, beautifully embroidered top, skirt and trimmings on the sleeves and collar are of high luster Baronet rayon. Kick pleat in front of skirt for added style, castillian red, black, Copenhagen blue.

High Grade
All Silk Satin
Crepe
35Z810
$17⁹⁵
POST. FREE

All Silk
Satin
Crepe
35Z811
$14⁹⁸
POST. FREE

Hand Beaded
on Metal Lace

All silk satin crepes are in style in prints or solids, complete with ornamental tassels, flowers, and rich embroidery. Cocoa, titian (new shade of golden rust), black, nickel gray, or blonde.

Every stitch of these two imported dresses is done by hand! Straight line slip over English broadcloth, Copenhagen blue, tan, or orchid. Imported voile, with dainty rows of hand drawn work and softly gathered Val lace outlining neck and sleeves. White, Copenhagen blue, or orchid.

Finest all silk satin crepe features color contrasting panels and pretty lace collar and cuffs, black-with-titian or cocoa-with-tan. All silk crepe satin dress with appliquéd embroidery and pipings of self material finish the front, neck, kimono sleeves, and flounces. Black, Titian, or blonde. Youthful, becoming sleeveless dress of lustrous all silk crepe with smart embroidery and rear tying self sash. Black, cocoa, or titian.

All silk satin crepe with smooth satin side alternating with panels of crepe, kimono sleeves with turn-back cuffs, black, cocoa, or nickel gray. Good quality all silk charmeuse frock with straight apron front simulated by reverse strips of self material edged with bands of contrasting color. Black with titian contrast, Navy blue with titian, or cocoa with tan.

All wool tweed flannel, youthful lines, tailored simplicity. Durable, finely woven straight line dress with becoming boyish round collar and turn-back cuffs, tan or powder blue with contrasting color checks. Ensemble costume of silk faille and silk print straight out of Paris, handsome jacket with delicate silk dress. Black, blonde, or titian.

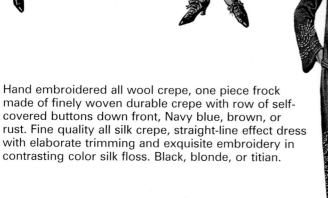

Hand embroidered all wool crepe, one piece frock made of finely woven durable crepe with row of self-covered buttons down front, Navy blue, brown, or rust. Fine quality all silk crepe, straight-line effect dress with elaborate trimming and exquisite embroidery in contrasting color silk floss. Black, blonde, or titian.

Silk-warp crepe in a printed pattern, grosgrain ribbon bow, beige with blue dots, beige with brown dots, gray with blue dots. All wool twill ensemble dress with fancy printed silk crepe giving the effect of a complete dress underneath. Navy blue. Imported non-crushable linen with front trimmed with tucks from neck to hem and large pearl buttons, exceptional value. Leather tan, Copenhagen blue, or green.

A most exquisite frock, lustrous silk georgette crepe over a seco silk slip and trimmed with hand beaded design in crystal and colored beads. Slight fullness over hips. Almond green, powder blue, or peach.

New York Styled!

One of This Season's Style Hits!

All Silk Crepe Satin— 35Z866 $14.98 Post. FR

MADE AND EMBROIDERED ENTIRELY BY HAND

English Broadcloth 35Z865 $7.95 Postage FREE

HAND EMB'D.

All Silk Pongee 42Z799 $2.98 Postage FREE

All Silk Crepe Satin 35Z867 $24.95 Postage FREE

All Silk Crepe Satin 35Z868 $14.98 Post FREE

Descriptions On Opposite Page!

Bellas Hess Pays All The Postage!

English broadcloth, imported voile, linen, and all silk crepe satin styles with elaborate embroidery, buckles, and rhinestones for effect for the demure woman. New York styled. Sweet and soft, all silk pongee panti-dress for the little lady, genuine Puerto Rican hand made and hand embroidered gowns of fine quality Nainsook in charming pastel shades, square neck, and dainty colored hand embroidery.

Imported voile, every stitch made by hand. Exquisite hand embroidery and hand drawn work elaborate the front, back, and sleeves. Orchid, Copenhagen blue, or white.

Tailored one-piece ensemble effect dress, non-crushable imported linen, wears and washes splendidly, simulated coat is held in position at waistline with linked buttons, Leather tan, orchid, or Copenhagen blue. One piece, straight-line model with beautiful hand drawn work, new style collar and cuffs of elbow sleeves, leather tan, Copenhagen blue, and green. Rich, lustrous knitted fibre silk with self and white raised cords through weave creating a checked pattern, neat little silk braid tie with two small ornaments at the end. Navy blue, black, or brown.

All silk crepe, all wool twill and silk ensemble, and English broadcloth tailored dresses. Beautiful embroidery and modern style collars and sleeves for any occasion. Black with titian, blonde with cocoa, Navy blue with titian, powder blue, peach, or orchid.

Handsome draped frock, unusual tunic front with vari-colored silk and metallic embroidery, rows of self covered buttons extend up plaits in front, Navy blue, black, or titian. Stunning new ensemble dress has the appearance of a two piece suit. Fine all wool twill with contrasting color silk crepe front. Heavily and richly ornamented bottom of tunic with Parisian silk embroidery. Navy blue with cocoa.

Silk, wool, satin, flannel… the most luxurious materials used to create trendy New York Fifth Avenue styles!

Popular new, handsome gown of lustrous, finest grade silk charmeuse, appliquéd embroidered net edges short sleeves, sash of self material. Black, Navy blue, or cocoa. Silk printed crepe dress in pretty all-over design, band of solid color silk crepe trimmed with covered buttons from shoulder to hem. Navy blue with tan pattern, tan with cocoa pattern, or gray with Copenhagen blue pattern.

Tunic frock, lustrous quality silk satin crepe. Deep all-around border of beautiful embroidery. Round neck, short sleeves and front opening with metallic cloth binding. Black with red embroidery, black with royal blue, titian with beige.

High Grade,

Hand embroidered heavy quality all silk crepe, satin crepe dresses with slenderizing lines for stout women in the most fashionable styles.

All Wool Twill and All Silk Satin Crepe 357930 $21.50 POST FREE

Novelty Embroidered

Heavy quality all silk French flat crepe trimmed with appliquéd embroidery of silk floss. Gray, powder blue, blonde. Two-piece ensemble costume, stunning, separate three-quarter length coat of fine all wool twill and complete one-piece all silk crepe dress. Navy blue twill with tan silk crepe. All silk satin crepe with rich metallic thread embroidery, black with jade green or Navy blue with titian.

Slim looking styles for stout women. Styled on long, straight slenderizing lines and made of lustrous fibre silk jersey with durable texture. Silk and metallic vari-colored thread embroidery ornaments. Black, Navy blue, or brown. Smart frock with long line effect cleverly carried out by fine plaits extending from bust to bottom of skirt, durable quality printed voile. Black, gray, or tan with harmonizing printed effects.

Fibre Silk Jersey
35Z940
$6.59
Postage FREE

Satin Faced Crepe and Chenille
35Z942
$10.98
POST. FREE.

Add a hat to a non-crushable linen, silk satin crepe or heavy silk lace frock, and hit the streets in New York style!

Canton crepe is smartly combined with silk ripple chenille crepe, novelty buttons and side belt of canton silk across the hips holds front and back panels in position. Black, Navy blue, cocoa.

All silk satin crepe, fine quality voile dresses are ornamented with beads and delicate embroidery. Black, Navy blue, cocoa, brown, orchid, beige.

Imported non-crushable real linen in fine, crisp, even weave. One piece dress styled on straight lines with tucks and pleats to give necessary fullness. White edging finishes collar and cuffs, all around self sash. Copenhagen blue, leather tan, peach, or orchid.

Non-crushable linen, high grade all silk crepe and all silk crepe satin dresses for looking beautiful, perfect for evening wear. Rhinestones, buttons, beads, sashes make the perfect finishing touches.

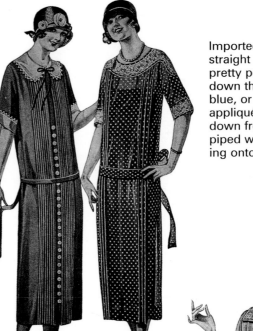

Imported non-crushable pure linen, straight slender lines accentuated by pretty pearl buttons between fine tucks down the front. Leather tan, Copenhagen blue, or white. Straight-line frock of appliquéd voile. Full-length tucks extend down front, handsome pattern Venise lace piped with voile to form yoke and extending onto sleeves. Navy blue, jade green.

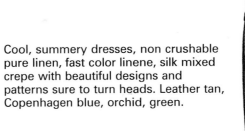

Cool, summery dresses, non crushable pure linen, fast color linene, silk mixed crepe with beautiful designs and patterns sure to turn heads. Leather tan, Copenhagen blue, orchid, green.

Hand Drawn Hand Embroidered Hand Sewn

Hand Drawn Hand Embroidered Hand Sewn

English Broadcloth 4Z100 $5.65 POST FREE

Imported pure linen, Roman striped English broadcloth, even Puerto Rican model frocks, stylish and becoming, stripes and solids for the debutante.

"Fade Not"

Plaided
English
Broadcloth
4Z151
$4.98
POST.FREE

English
Broadcloth
4Z152
$4.39
POST.FREE

Hand Embroidered

English broadcloth, highly mercerized rajah cloth, or appliquéd dotted voile styles, pretty and proper, with bows and buttons to adorn. Tan, powder blue, orchid, almond green, tangerine, green.

Guaranteed fast color linene with stylish front panel formed by rows of silk fagoting and trimming of white pique on collar, cuffs, and pockets. Leather tan, Copenhagen blue, or orchid. English broadcloth, fine and silky in striking plaid design with trimming down front with two broad bias folds set off by handsome pearl buttons. White ground with blue, tangerine, or green plaids. Hand embroidery on dress of English broadcloth, long sleeves with turn-back button-trimmed cuffs. Powder blue, orchid, or tan,

"Fade Not" Guaranteed Fast Color

Mercerized English Print
4Z172
$2.79
POST. FREE

Good Quality Striped Gingham
4Z180
$1.69
POST FREE

Printed Linene
4Z182
$1.29
POST FREE

"Fade Not" Guaranteed Fast Color Linene
4Z181
$2.98
POST. FREE

Linene, mercerized pongee, mercerized English print, striped English broadcloth, buttons used to decorate and dazzle, popular turn-back collar on most styles.

Because a woman is large is no reason why she should not be dressed smartly and becomingly. Striped gingham or fast color and printed linene frocks are excellently styled for dressy occasions, but are also perfectly suitable for home requirements.

Imported, semi-made dresses, imported non-crushable linen and imported voile. Simple directions for completing the garment are included.

Non-Crushable Imported Pure Linen
4Z191
$5.49
POST. FREE

English Broadcloth
4Z193
$4.98
POST. FREE

Designed to give slenderizing lines to women of full figure, these gorgeous styles give confidence and satisfaction to the wearer! Imported gingham, non-crushable imported pure linen, appliquéd dotted voile, or English broadcloth, all soft, durable, and excellent for summertime fun.

Fibre Silk Bengalette
2Z725
$2.89
Postage FREE

Brocaded Pattern All Silk Crepe De Chine
2Z726
$5.98
Postage FREE

Very Fine Quality Linen

Very Fine Quality Linen

EXTRA MATERIAL FOR COLLAR & FACING
45Z521
$4.95
POSTAGE FREE

Fibre silk bengalette tunic, collar, cuffs and trimming band at the edge are of contrasting color braid in filet design. Fallow tan, Navy blue, powder blue. Tunic of embossed crepe de Chine in brocaded pattern, front trimmed with novel pearl buttons, titian, fallow tan, gray.

Very chic and becoming new all silk flat crepe frock with Parisian version of the dolman sleeve, Cracklehead blue and Lanvin Green, woven plaid outfit, dress has a tucked batiste blouse and plaid skirt with inverted pleats, black and white. Two-piece all silk flat crepe dress, Seco bodice top and box pleated skirt. Mother Goose Tan or Channel Red. Figured rayon with popular wide bands of shirring. Lace collar and bosom with plain color rayon underlay. Rose, Gracklehead Blue, or Green.

Pretty all silk flat crepe dress with bloused bolero, shimmery rayon crepe with diagonal tucked sleeves and blouse, flowered and printed all silk crepe de Chine, brocaded rayon crepe with embroidered underbodice, all silk Georgette crepe, and tiny flowered print silk and cotton crepes are very pretty dresses for spring and summer wear.

Very chic and becoming small womens and junior miss dresses of Radium tub-silk frock, printed silk and cotton crepe, plain and printed crepe de Chine, and all silk embroidered flat crepe.

Stylishly effective misses' dresses, in rayon crepe trimmed with narrow bandings of contrasting color, crepe de Chines with fluttering picoted handkerchief panels on the skirt, and all wool flannel. Colors bright and bold for summer excitement – tan with green, Grackle with tan, tangerine, Copenhagen blue, gray, and rose.

Handsome plaid rayon and crepe frock in peach or Gracklehead blue can be worn in any season. Neat and tailored linen frock (also in high lustered rayon) with white linen-piped yoke and bosom front. Copenhagen blue, tan, lavender, or rose.

Smartly tailored all silk flat crepe frock with trim tailored collar and cuffs. Roman-striped satin ribbon and silk cord and tassel at the neck finish the look. Rose and Copenhagen blue. Stunning two-piece frock, polka dot tub silk frock with V-neck and pleated skirt attached to a Seco bodice top. Navy with tan dots, tan with Navy dots.

Slim tailored all wool check tweed flannel with trig boyish collar and turn-back cuffs and wide leather belt. Tan with blue plaid and blue belt or powder blue with tan plaid and tan belt. Draped model of all silk satin crepe with supple texture and rich luster, corresponding ornament on right side catches a narrow belt and chic bow. Black, titian, or gray. Lustrous silk faille with lustrous woven rayon in a beautiful all over pattern, plaited skirt, narrow belt, fancy buttons with loops at neck.

All Silk Crepe with New Button Embroidery Done Entirely by Hand 35Z920 $19.98 POST. FREE

All Silk Georgette over Seco Slip 35Z922 $14.98 POST. FREE

All Silk Satin Crepe 35Z923 $14.98 POST. FREE

English broadcloth dress, band of self material finely tucked, row of pearl buttons on stylish vestee. Tan, powder blue, or orchid. Fashionable straight slender lines, rich embroidery, and a cleverly designed trimming that suggest this popular all silk crepe satin tunic effect dress is a hit for the season! Black with king blue, titian with tan, or silver gray with blue.

Latest dresses from Paris, perfect for spring and summer, silk georgette, wool flannel, and printed silk, or silk crepe. Embroidered and decorated in the highest fashion. Navy blue, cocoa, gray, Arab (shade between ashes of roses and brick), powder blue, tan, jade green, maize, royal blue, and black.

Specially designed for stylish misses of youthful figure who demand the most distinctive New York models! Imported non-crushable linen, all silk georgette over silk slip, imported voile, and all silk satin crepe styles for every occasion. Hand drawn details.

All Wool Tweed Flannel
80 Z 745
$6.98
POST. FREE

Imported Non Crushable Linen and Eyelet Embroidery
80 Z 746
$5.98
POST. FREE

All Silk Canton Crepe
80 Z 747
$9.98
POST. FREE

English Broadcloth Ensemble Dress
80 Z 748
$4.98
POST. FREE

Smart, girlish models in all wool tweed flannel, imported non-crushable linen and eyelet embroidery, all silk canton crepe, and English broadcloth.

In the smart, exclusive dress shops in New York City, you could not find a handsomer frock, all silk satin crepe with four double ruffles and tiny self covered buttons running the length. Almond green, black, or tan. Silk floss interspersed with gilt tinsel thread in this lovely all silk satin crepe. Blonde, cocoa, titian, or black. One piece ensemble dress made of fine all wool twill with all silk crepe front giving the appearance of an entire separate dress underneath. Navy blue with cranberry red front.

All Silk
Satin
Crepe
8OZ750
$14.98
POST. FREE

Hand Drawn
Pure
Linen
8OZ765
$4.98
POSTAGE
FREE

ALL WOOL
Tweed
Flannel
8OZ766
$5.98
POSTAGE
FREE

Flowered
Appliqued
Voile
8OZ767
$3.29
POSTAGE
FREE

Striped
English
Broadcloth
8OZ768
$4.98
POSTAGE
FREE

Stylish dresses of pure Irish linen, all wool tweed (plaid), appliquéd voile, and striped English broadcloth in gorgeous spring and summer shades will show off the beauty of the misses' figure!

Fine Quality
All Silk
Crepe
8OZ757
$14.98
POST. FREE

Becoming! Distinctive! Modish, straight-line tailored frock of high grade all wool tan flannel with vari-colored Roman stripes and harmonizing trim. Parisian styles favor appliqués and two-tone novelty trimming, as displayed in this all silk satin crepe frock with silk velvet edging. Powder blue, titian, or blonde. Loose flowing knife plaited panels give fashionable flare and accent along with a stylish low waistline in an all silk crepe dress. Blonde, almond green, or black.

Fast color linene, English broadcloth, high luster rajah pongee, non-crushable linen dresses, rich embroidery designs, lazy daisy, French knots, and daring stitches. Leather tan, orchid, Copenhagen blue, peach, green, and white.

English Broadcloth
80Z773
$2⁹⁸
POST. FREE

High Lustre Rajah Pongee
40Z327
$1⁸⁹
POST. FREE

Fade-Not Fast Color Linene
40Z329
$1⁰⁰
POST. FREE

Dainty summery dresses, silk soutache embroidery down the front of imported English broadcloth. Powder blue, peach, or apple green. Self flounces arranged in three tiers on a frock of two-tone printed silk mixed crepe. Navy with tan pattern, tan with Copenhagen blue pattern, or Copenhagen blue with tan pattern. A dress of sheer voile with pleats on the entire front in an accordion pleated effect, monk collar of sheer white organdy and edged with Val lace. Miami (the new shade of apricot), maize, or green. English broadcloth frock with self material collar and cuffs on elbow length sleeves, lace trimmed. Powder blue, peach, or orchid.

Costume tunics in the best fabrics, novelty fibre silk, crepe de Chine, printed silk, silk Spanish lace, and hand beaded rayon. Wear a plain skirt underneath and these prêt-a-porte tunics will keep you dressed to impress!

All Over Printed Silk
2Z706
$4⁹⁸
Post. FREE

Hand Beaded All Silk Crepe De Chine
2Z710
$9⁹⁸
Post FREE

Silk Spanish Lace & Crepe De Chine
2Z709
$5²⁹
Post FREE

Slenderizing styles for stout figures. Woven gingham apron dress, linene, charmeuse, and striped broadcloth morning dresses, exceptional comfort while still offering a modish look with long lines.

Why wear your best garments when you can protect them with these washable woven morning dresses? Plaid gingham, rayon gingham, novelty suiting, cotton foulard, and cotton pongee styles.

More than just an ordinary housedress, these styles offer attractive patterns and colors, polka dots, stripes, and embroidered effects, topped with ribbons and ties to add flair.

Special value

Bargain

Hand Embroidered Serpentine Crepe
23 H C6529
$1 88

Fast Printed Pongee
23 H C6526
$1 79

Percale
23 H C6519
$1 29 Up

Genuine Broadcloth Hoover Style Apron
23 H C6547
98¢

Charleston morning dress, chambray, fancy printed material belt, blue, green lavender. Broadcloth hoover style April dress, reversible, white, blue, lavender, honeydew. Polka dotted apron dress of percale, black bow accentuates V-neck, Navy blue.

Comfortable housedresses… in hand embroidered Amoskeag chambray, cotton charmeuse, printed pongee, striped woven gingham, broadcloth, Japanese-style serpentine crepe, in lively colors and patterns.

Youthful frock of all silk flat crepe, shirred panel on skirt, girdle finished with novelty buckle. Wide dolman sleeves with fitted cuffs, and deep Paris "V" neck piped with paisley and topped off with a smart silk flower.

High grade all silk crepe ensemble costume. Dress of good quality lustrous all silk printed crepe, straight-line model with fullness held at sides by elastic shirring. Becoming youthful collar and jabot is finished with grosgrain bow. Coat is of high grade all wool flannel, three button front closing and novel cuffs with buttons. The very last word in style! Ashes of roses (a new shade between salmon and brick), powder blue, or tan.

All Silk
Crepe
Satin
80Z725
$12.98
POST.FREE

Left:
All silk satin crepe, embroidered in colorful shades of silk floss. Double two-tone all silk crepe collar and cuffs in pastel shades adds smartness. Black, titian, almond green. For real Parisian style and smartness, a straight-line, sleeveless dress, styled to give the fashionable silhouette, made from all silk satin crepe. Very chic French touches are seen in the three ruffles of self material across bottom of frock. Cocoa, titian, or black.

Right:
Up-to-the-minute cross word puzzle print of fine quality all silk crepe. Stylish slip-over model with fancy pleated ruffle all the way down from shoulder to hem. Blue with beige cross-word pattern, red with beige, or black with white.

All silk satin crepe, all wool flannel, imported voile dresses that smart young women of New York favor! And straight from France, styled after the "Mon Lapin" (my rabbit) dress, a frock with a little bunny in captivating embroidery and velvety chenille fringe around bottom.

All Silk
Satin
Crepe
8 O Z 731
$13.98
POST. FREE

Mon Lapin
(MY RABBIT)
Parisian
Dress of
All Wool
Flannel!
8 O Z 736
$16.98
POST. FREE

Porch frocks and cottage dresses, perfect for a lazy Sunday afternoon. Checked or striped gingham, printed linene, soft beach cloth, with fancy stitching on collar, sleeves, and front. Aprons of percale, linene, cretonne trimming, sturdy and durable for the hard working wife and mother.

Hand Embroidered

Hand Embroidered

Good Quality Gingham
4Z201
$1.98
POST. FREE

Hand Painted Linene
4Z204
$1.98
POST. FREE

Good Quality Gingham
4Z203
98¢
POST. FREE

Plain and Check Linene
4Z211
98¢
POST. FREE

Fine Quality Fancy Percale
4Z214
79¢
POST. FREE

Plain and Check Linene
4Z215
98¢
POST. FREE

Sportswear and Separates

High Grade
All Wool Twill
Silk Crepe Lined
1 Z 322
28⁵⁰
POST FREE

Slenderizing lines are most desirable this season, especially in the full-figured woman's suits.

Ensemble costumes are the latest rage... all wool twill and heavy silk crepe or all silk faille combine with beautiful rich hand embroidery, ornate buttons, and silk braid trimmings to create the perfect effect!

All wool poiret twill, well tailored suit with mannish collar finished with silk tassels, handsome embroidery appearing on collar, sleeves, and bottom, Navy blue. All wool pin checked homespun tweed with Johnny collar adorned with wide panel of vari-color braid in tapestry effect design, tan or gray color pin check. Sport suit of all wool flannel, sport skirt with kick plait in front, sleeveless jacket with large patch pockets. Powder blue, tan, or ashes of roses.

Distinctive and smart looking all wool flannel with wrap-around slenderizing style and the very new Peter Pan skirt, both featured in New York's finest shops!

Stylish man tailored ensemble suits for misses, in all silk crepe, all wool twill, and all wool flannel tweed. Stunning worn with or without a coat. Fine garments for the hard working woman.

Peter Pan Skirt

High Grade

All Wool
Striped
Flannel
3Z820
$4.98
POST. FREE

All Wool
Flannel
3Z821
$4.98
Post. FREE

All Wool
Tweed Flannel
3Z841
$2.98
POST. FREE

The favorite material for spring, silk crepe faille, features a rich luster. This skirt is fashioned with graceful all 'round knife plaits, side closing, and self-belt in tan, navy blue, or gray.

This season, fashion says SKIRTS! All wool striped flannel and blocked polaire are featured in the smartest styles approved for spring. Side button style features handmade buttonholes and one convenient slash pocket. Plaited skirt is slenderizing following the demand by present fashions.

Skirts styled for New York women. Plaited, made of silk crepe faille, styled in alternating large and small box plaits pressed to remain in position. Gray, tan, or powder blue. Handsome skirt of all wool tweed flannel in rich, wonderful plaids, finished with buttons and hand made buttonholes. Blue or tan. All wool crepe or all wool tweed flannel knife plaited skirts, suitable for sports, dress, and general wear. Gray, tan, Navy blue, black, white.

Stunning suits for misses… same styles that you find on Fifth Avenue! All wool poiret twill, home-spun tweed, or all wool flannel. Johnny collar long length jackets, well tailored skirt with side closing, deep patch pockets.

Stylish slenderizing skirts, dressy silk crepe faille fashioned on long, graceful lines and alternating box and side plaits. Sport satin skirt, two side pockets, side closing belt of self material. Plaited skirt, all wool crepe, self covered buttons, belt of self material.

Smart looking overblouses, buttons and fancy fasteners for the most up-to-date looks.

Misses skirts, plaited or smooth, stripes, solids, all wool worsted, silk crepe faille, tweed flannel.

Brushed wool sports coat, fancy knit windbreaker, wool worsted ribbed knit sweater, and ribbed knit sweater coats with delightful rayon designs, stripes, and embroidered decorations.

Style - wise women who demand correct sports togs are wearing these beautiful Brushed Wool Coats. All edges and the two pockets are bound with contrasting color unbrushed wool. An embroidered motif in monogram effect is appliqued on. Of Wool with cotton back for service. Sizes: 36 to 44. Order Sweater 2 inches larger than actual Bust measure. State Size.
22 H 7104 Buff
22 H 7105 Silver Gray
22 H 7106 Poudre Blue
PRICE, Each.... $2.95 Postage, 10c Extra

You'll see these fancy knit Windbreakers at country clubs and vacation resorts, for the stunning block pattern with Rayon design is dashing and colorful. Made of All Wool Worsted with a thread of cotton for added service. The pocket tops and the ribbed cuffs and hip band are in solid color. Sizes: 34 to 44. Order Sweater 2 inches larger than actual Bust measure. State Size.
22 H 7127 Poudre Blue
22 H 7128 Buff
22 H 7129 Jockey Red
PRICE, Each.... $2.98 Postage, 8c Extra

$4.98

Sport and outing clothes for the active lady. Knicker suits or skirt suits worn with or without jacket offer incredible style and exceptional comfort. Tan, gray, powder blue.

Sportswear blouses and sweaters, printed or plain are all the rage in New York.

Tunics and blouses for the New York woman. Beautiful chenille embroidery, cotton crepe prints, pleated cotton pongee or striped cotton broadcloth. Stunning tailoring for slenderizing and complementary lines.

Silk, English broadcloth, dimity, and viole dress up these over blouses. Most feature elaborate hand embroidery and hand drawn work. All are attractive and long wearing. White, tan, or gold, orchid and blue stripes.

English broadcloth blouses, with pretty trimming and decoration. Practical and attractive for sports or every day wear. White, tan, powder blue.

45

Regulation middy of strong, durable Lonsdale jean is cleverly cut with sloping sides, white or khaki. Good quality tan cotton pongee overblouse with narrow tucks trimming the front, and crisp white dimity over blouse with collar and turn-back cuffs finished with a silk cord.

All Worsted Brushed Very Smart 32Z806 $4.79 POST FREE

Smart swagger sport coat of soft, fluffy Angora wool worsted. Cross-striping in contrasting color, two button fastening at neck and bottom. Silver with navy blue or buff with brown. Fashionable "Kid boots" style of heavy quality fibre silk in a long wearing tricot weave, soft and lustrous. Powder blue, silver, or gold. Attractive sweater in the Fair Isles design, soft pleasing worsted blend with brilliant fibre silk in striking three color Jacquard effect. Buff, powder blue, or silver.

Wool Worsted and Fibre Silk 32Z821 $1.98 POST FREE

Stylish new models for warmth and comfort, all wool check flannel, angora-finished brushed wool, jersey-ribbed all wool worsted tuxedo styles, buff, powder blue, white, jade green, black.

All
Worsted
Softly
Brushed
32Z833
$4.98
POST.FREE

Worsted
Fibre Silk
Trimmed
32Z832
$3.98
POST.FREE

Soft Quality

All
Worsted
32Z834
$2.98
Girlish
Model

All Wool
Worsted
32Z835
$3.49
POST.FREE

Genuine Bargain

All Wool
32Z851
$2.98
POST.FREE

Fine Ribbed
Worsted
32Z852
$2.98
POST.FREE

Fine Ribbed
All Worsted
32Z854
$1.89
POST.FREE

Worsted
Checked Front
32Z855
$1.98

Sweaters for young women, perfect for school or everyday wear. Lovely sleeveless fibre silk Piccadilly front sweater,

Beautiful sweaters, smart and becoming in the latest patterns and weaves, mannish styles are popular in the softest, yet most durable fashions and bright, new colors.

Knickers, of twill, cotton tweed, all wool tweed flannel, and pure linen – just the thing for riding, hiking, golfing, or driving. Solids and plaids, for any attitude!

3Z874. Women are sharing equally with men these days in the enjoyment of outdoor life. There is scarcely any form of outdoor sports in which they are not participating. To get the fullest enjoyment from this pastime, however, one must be appropriately and smartly attired. Here is an unusually good opportunity to get shapely, well tailored Knickers—just the thing for riding, hiking, golfing or driving at just about what the material alone would cost you. Made of high grade, closely woven All Wool Tweed. Side closing; two inset pockets. Adjustable buttoned knee bands. Buckle trimmed belt drawn through loops of self material. Reinforced seat. Beautifully tailored; faultlessly finished. Tan or gray Tweed mixtures. Sizes: 25 to 36 inches waist measure. **$2.98**
Postage Paid To Your Door.

Styled right for dress wear, yet practical enough for sports. These separates of high grade wool flannel will get you through the day, whatever your task. Skirt features plaits and handmade buttonholes for just the right fit.

3Z869
Khaki Twill
$1 89
3Z870
Cotton Tweed
$1 98
POST. FREE.

Pure Linen
Also In
Solid White
$2 98
POST. FREE.

Outerwear

$19⁹⁸

$7⁹⁸

Charming coats for the miss and small woman. Typical of what the smartly dressed young woman is wearing on the avenue. Coats are all wool in poiret sheen, velour, and suede velour with braid or fur trim. All are lined throughout with sateen.

Daringly original designs, smart and stylish. College styles, each with a girlish flair. Stunning coats for young women.

Ultra stylish spring weight velour coat with leopard fur fabric trimming. Poiret sheen coat with silk braid applied in smart lattice, trimming repeated on cuffs and deep side pocket.

Typical miss and small women's coats, all wool velour, poiret sheen with Coney fur edging, fancy check and all wool polo, in smart colors for spring.

Fur trimming is all the rage this season, but fancy embroidery will always do the trick for fashion!

$6.98

$6.95

$6.98

$7.49

$9.95

All silk black satin, all wool rust, tan, or poudre blue velour, and Navy blue, gray, and tan all wool poiret sheen coats, trimmed with summer fur. Marvelous style and couture.

$7.98 $4.98

Even in warm weather, these wool coats provide cool comfort.
Suede velour and poiret sheen guarantee excellent wear.

14^{98}

11^{98}

Stepping out in style has never been so fun! Dazzling and delightfully colorful, these wool dress and sport coats mimic the highest New York fashions of the day!

Sometimes the simpler styles are the most becoming, and sometimes the trimming is quite irresistible, as demonstrated in lovely summer wool poiret sheen and velour coats.

All wool velour coat, tan, gracklehead blue, rust, button-trimming side panels and soft fluffy moufflon fur. Chic straight line coat, tan, rust, gray, with modish collar, facing, and cuffs of smart popular fur fabric. All wool velour coat with clever braided trimming and uniquely embroidered pockets and collar, gracklehead blue, gray, and rosewood.

Stunning summer styles, velour, wool, poiret sheen models with summer coney fur trimming or attractive soutache braid and velour decorations.

$12.98

Charming coats for misses and small women, flattering and chic. Fur lined collars, lined throughout with lustrous satinette, gracklehead blue, palmetto green, tan, and rust.

Youthfully styled and slenderizing all wool coats are sateen lined and feature summer moufflon or summer coney fur trim. The tailoring is exceptionally well executed and is a great value. Green, gray, rust, and tan.

Stylish coats for full figures. These coats insure a smart, slim line. Coats of all wool poiret sheen, velour, and moire silk all lined in satin de chine. Rust, tan, gray, and cracklehead blue.

Graceful coats for full figures. These coats, of Moire silk and velour are for distinguished women everywhere. Attractively trimmed with summer fur and silk braid, these coats will be worn for practically every occasion.

6^{98}

6^{95}

7^{98} 4^{98}

Typical girls and juniors coats feature novelty checks, elaborate silk embroidery, silk floss stitching, and contrasting collar and cuffs all in stunning color combinations to enhance the youthful styling. Cracklehead blue, cranberry, rosewood, and tan.

6^{98}

7^{49}

9^{95}

The smart, pretty styling of these coats will surely make any young miss feel grown up. All wool coats take young women anywhere in style. Featuring distinctive details include long shawl collars, summer coney fur trims, buttons, silk braids, and gathering at the waist. In poudre blue, rosewood, cranberry, rust, and tan.

High Lustre
Boliva
Full Lined
5Z150
19^{98}
POST. FREE

High Grade

All Wool
Chamois
Suede
Full Lined
5Z151
19^{98}
POST. FREE

Styled and tailored in New York. High lustre Boliva wool, chamois suede, and downy weave coats in all the big city styles. Deep, rich, velvety trims, contrasting piping, and silk floss stitching enhance these latest, most sought after styles.

Stunning coat of all wool chamois suede, finely woven, tailored on fashionable straight lines. Collar of fine quality white summer fur, wide sleeves trimmed with silk, floss stitching ,and buttons. Arab, Lanvin green, or tan.

All Wool
Chamois
Suede
Full
Lined
5 Z I 8 I
22.50
POST-FREE

High Grade

High Grade

Look as pretty going as you do coming! These specially tailored stylish coats feature inverted plaits, tailored panels, pin tucks, and hand embroidered silk stitching. Navy blue, tan, or gray.

All wool bengallette, a soft finished woven cross ribbed fabric with becoming summer fur trim and lined with satin striped radium. Arab or tan. Fine quality, high luster Bolivia cut on stylish lines with the popular Johnny collar and turn-back cuffs. Black, gray, or tan.

Handsome new spring cape, made of high luster wool Bolivia with beautiful soft thick pile, large collar of moufflon fur, trimmed with coiled rosette of colored self material. Black with gray fur or tan with tan fur. Smart cording outlined by silk braid emphasizes this stylish coat, made from all wool Kashmir polaire, with a lovely lustrous camel's hair finish. Tan, Arab, or gray.

5 Z 130
$14.98
POSTAGE FREE

High Grade
All Wool
Twill
5 Z 1251
$22.50
POST. FREE

High Grade
All Wool
Flannel
5 Z 126
$15.98
POST. FREE

Slender silhouette popular "stand-up" collar, square set-in shoulders and new puff sleeves in a tailored spring coat of all wool poiret twill. Navy blue or tan. Straight-line wrap in smooth all wool flannel with full lining of fine silk crepe, Johnny collar, and handsome buttons fastening front. Tan, Arab, or powder blue.

All wool Lochmoor polaire overplaid coat, Johnny collar, cuffs, and sides decorated with polaire bands and self covered buttons. Genuine summer Moufflon collar perfects a smooth all wool flannel coat lined with silk warp crepe. Another stunning coat, all wool Poiret twill with appliquéd Duvetyn trimming and summer squirrel fur collar with hand embroidery.

Dressy brocaded silk bengaline coat,
stunning wool Bolivia coat, or mannish
tailored all wool polaire coat.

High
Luster
Bolivia
Full Lined
5 Z 161
$16.98
POST. FREE

All wool blocked polaire, velour, and kashmir polaire
styles, each fully lined for warmth and comfort.

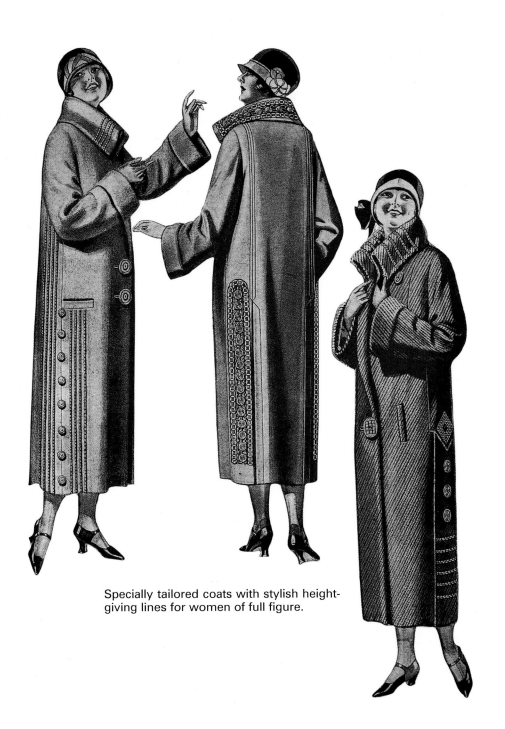

High Grade

High Grade

All Wool Chamois Suede Crepe Lined 5 Z 1 4 5 $24.95 POST. FREE

All Wool Blocked Polaire Full Lined 5 Z 1 4 6 $12.98 POST. FREE

Tucking, one of the most effective style trimmings of the season, is used with stunning effect in these fashionable tailored coats.

Specially tailored coats with stylish height-giving lines for women of full figure.

Summer Fur Trimmed

All wool flannel, all wool Kashmir polaire, all wool velour, and crepe lined coats trimmed with summer fur.

The Popular New Coating

Well woven all wool polaire, tucked pockets trimmed with straps of self material, popular Johnny collar, polo tan or gray. Beautiful luxurious all wool bengalette, deep fur collar of genuine Moufflon, soft and silky, Arab or tan. All wool dressy velour with wide tinsel-and-silk braid and Bobby collar. Arab, tan, and gray.

Coats and capes for the stylish New York woman, creative and attractive embroidery and buttons add flare.

High Grade

All Wool Flannel Crepe Lined 8Z126 $16.98 POST. FREE

High luster wool bolivia and all wool velour make up some of the season's hottest coats and capes.

Becoming and pretty choker scarves, each with spring catch head and trimmed with paws and tail. Snow white erminette coney jackquette, turn over Johnny collar, and modish flare sleeves, finished with wind shields.

Spring jacquettes and summer furs, leopard coney, natural red fox, gray squirrel, thibateen natural lynx, and mink marmot scarves and shoals.

Fashionable raincoats for women and children in colored rubberized canton cloth, yellow oilskin, or rubberized sateen. Each can be trimmed with fur collars for that finishing touch.

Underwear

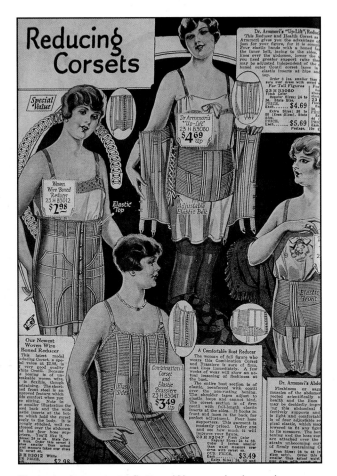

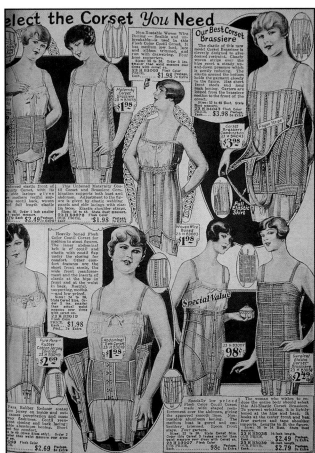

Reducing corsets to flatten. Woven wire boned reducer, combination corset, and elastic brassiere.

Para rubber reducers, flesh color coutil corsets, and all elastic corset brassieres for style, comfort, and health.

Up to the minute favored styles to improve figure. Four garter dobbie cloth brassieres for dance or sport use or when you're really busy at home.

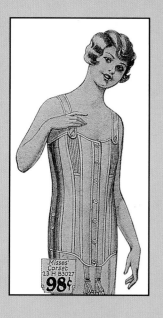

Misses'
Corset
23 H B3027
98¢

23 H B3024
98¢

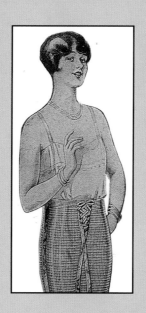

Coutil
Reducing
Corset
23 H B3016
$1.98

Batiste
Bust Form
Corset
23 H B3017
$1.98

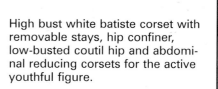

High bust white batiste corset with removable stays, hip confiner, low-busted coutil hip and abdominal reducing corsets for the active youthful figure.

Hip
Confiner
23 H B3048
98¢

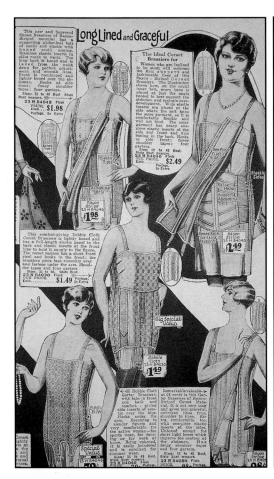

Long lined and graceful, ideal corset brassieres for women who are inclined to be stout and welcome firm support and fashionable lines. Dobbie cloth corset brassiere, lightly boned, hose supporters and garters.

Clever women choose these good quality rayon slips or tub silk costume slips which are all the vogue in New York. Pleated hips for slim fit. Henna, tan, green, black, white, Navy blue.

Striped Sateen
23 H A4346
98¢

Nainsook
23 H A4345
98¢

23 H A4351
98¢

Nainsook
23 H A4360
98¢

Shadow Proof Hem

For Stout Women

Shadow Proof Hem

23 H A4402
$1³⁵

Shadow Proof Hem

"Non Cling Magnolia Cloth"
23 H A4396
$1²⁵

Bargain
23 H A4401
89¢

23 H A4395
69¢

Shadow Proof Hem

Rayon
23 H A4390
$1²⁹

Dressy white nainsook costume slip with val and shadow lace decoration, striped sateen costume slip with accordion pleats, famous "fruit of the loom" muslin white costume slip, looks beautiful even underneath your highest fashion.

Chic spring styles, costume slips are more important than ever, for straight slim lines are still the vogue. Nainsook, "Magnolia cloth," Satinette… every style any woman desires!

Delightful rayon teddy, appealing envelope chemise in flesh, peach, or orchid offer tasteful individual style, sensual and enjoyable to wear. Puerto Rican hand embroidered and hand made two piece cotton pongee pajamas, cool and dainty, charming design of cross-stitch rosebuds and French knots trimming the pockets and collar.

Lace trimmed rayon vests with fancy braided shoulder straps, flesh, orchid, and peach. Cross bar nainsook two piece pajamas, refreshing for summer wear. Bands of contrasting nainsook form the shoulder, armhole, and bodice effect top. White, flesh.

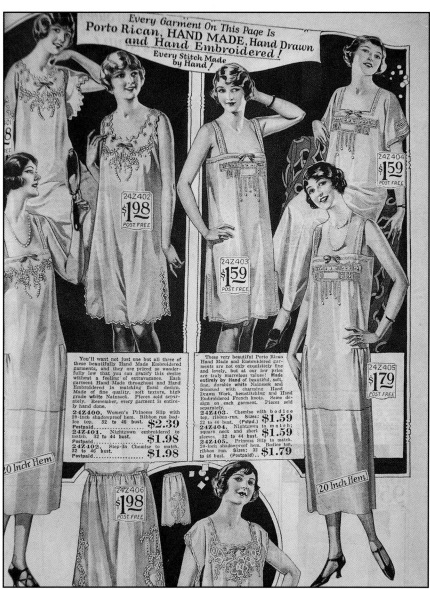

Puerto Rican hand made, hand drawn, and hand embroidered nightgowns and slips. White nainsook and batiste.

New sport model, latest union suit of fine elastic white ribbed cotton, provides utmost comfort. Built-up style or bodice top style.

Soft, lustrous seco silk with lustrous silk dots is used for two-piece pajamas, with fine quality val lace forming the trimming at neck, sleeves, and pants. Flesh or orchid. Lace provides the yoke and sleeves of a lovely gown of sheer white nainsook. Embroidered medallions and rosebuds garnish the front.

Seco Silk 24Z416 $179 POST.FREE

24Z421 98¢ POST.FREE

Pin Check Nainsook

Seco silk, pin check nainsook, bluebird and woven crepe pajamas and night gowns… look your best even in the restful hours. Smooth and soft – dreams have never been this sweet!

Cap 24Z433 69¢

24Z432 98¢ POST.FREE

Pincheck Nainsook 24Z437 89¢ POST.FREE

24Z431 $198 POST.FREE

Seco Silk 24Z436 $249 POST.FREE

24Z438 $149 POST.FREE

Women's slip-on style gowns, of crepe de Chine, longcloth, nainsook, and satin striped radium. Beautiful embroidery and delicate bows and ribbons for a unique finish.

Every woman needs a princess slip or elegant petticoat to accompany her favorite dress or suit.

Hand embroidered underwear is a must-have this season. Princess slip of white longcloth, gathered at sides to give desired fullness, hand embroidered and lace trimmed. Another princess slip of closely woven shadow stripe sateen, top finished with hemstitching, white, flesh, black, Navy blue, brown. Pretty boudoir cap of pink or blue satin and net trimmed with lace, satin plaiting.

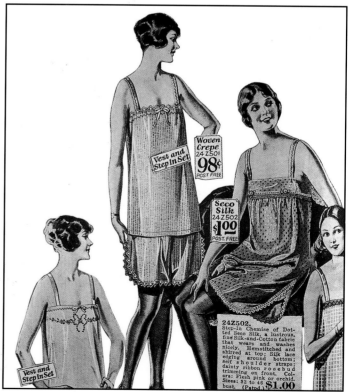

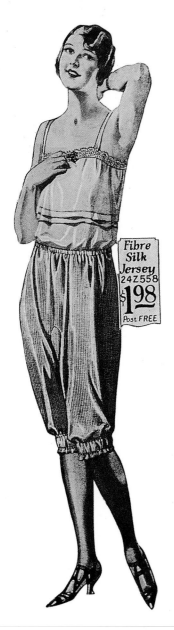

Fibre
Silk
Jersey
24Z558
$1.98
Post FREE

Woven Crepe
Blue Bird Design

24Z559
65¢
Post FREE

Sateen
24Z560
49¢
Post FREE

Hand
Embroidered
24Z556
45¢
Post FREE

Pincheck
Nainsook
24Z557
49¢
Post FREE

Step-ins and bloomers of woven crepe, fibre silk jersey, longcloth, batiste, satin striped rayon and durable cotton materials. Elastic waist for extra comfort.

Below:
Latest model bandeaus and brassieres for support and control. Extra heavy boning across front holds diaphragm firmly and comfortably in place. Bust support of white cotton mesh or cambric with embroidery yoke. Smooth, cool satin bandeau brassieres with filet lace top, shoulder straps.

24Z572
85¢
POST. FREE

DIAPHRAGM
REDUCER

DIAPHR
REDUC

EXTRA
SIZE

ELASTIC

ELASTIC

Genuine "Madam X Reducing Corset and Brassiere," made of authentic, steam cured Para rubber. Makes lines of a woman's figure appear longer and slimmer, and all the superfluous flesh on the waist, hips, and abdomen is gently massaged away, causing substantial reduction of weight, with back lacing to permit adjustment as the lady grows more slender!

Rubber diaphragm reducer, reducing brassieres, covered in Milanese silk, Sea Island stockinette. Provides excellent support. Front or back hook styles, heaving boning for added reinforcement, lace accents. Flesh pink.

Rubber Reducer Covered With Milanese Silk

23Z194 $5 89 POST.FREE

23Z211 $998

Rubber Reducing Brassiere, Covered W Sea Island Stockine

Front Hook Back Lace Para Rubber Reducer

23Z195 $3 79 POST.FREE

23Z199 $1 98 POST.FREE

23Z196 $3 95 POST.FREE

Rubber Reducing Brassiere, Covered With Sea Island Stocki

ELASTIC

23Z160 49¢ POST.FREE

For the many thousands of women who are today turning to the elastic corset, and a special abdomen reducer! Fleshy hips and midsection are straightened into modish lines and reduced with these comfortable corsets. Non-lacing, side or back fastening, embroidery trimmed tops. Flesh pink.

A variety of styles mostly for small and medium figures; summer net, misses corset, elastic brassieres of flesh pink brocade. Hose supporters, reducing girdles.

Firmly woven flesh pink brocade combination girdle and brassieres, diaphragm reducing corsettes, extra long or regular length, hose supporters, particularly well adapted for women of full figures.

Pantalettes, slips, and petticoats, in Japanese radium silk, shadow striped sateen, gingham, fibre silk jersey. Perfect for sleeping, or lounging about the house. High-lustre finish, good quality for durability and comfort. Black, Navy blue, brown, cocoa, tan, pink, white, green, and purple.

Ideal for wear under spring and summer dresses, princess slips, tunic slips, or petticoats in fibre silk jersey, Japanese radium silk, Habutai silk, cotton, and sateen. Cut full and roomy, well shaped, with ruffles and scallops to enhance.

Beautiful full fashioned silk stockings, mercerized lace effect yarn stockings, and chiffon weight hose of lustrous thread silk reinforced with fibre. Smooth and soft, perfect underneath your favorite dress, gives shapely lines and smart support.

Cotton
Canton Crepe
4Z222
$3.98
POST FREE

High Grade
Cotton
Canton Crepe
4Z224
$3.98
POST FREE

Handsome robes for restful hours! Luxurious materials used to fashion the most comfortable, lavish garments. Loose, flowing kimono sleeves, ornaments in contrasting colors for added effect. Rose, Copenhagen blue, peach, turquoise, honeydew.

4Z231
$3.95
POST FREE

Hand Embroidered
Silk Mixed
Crepe de Chine

Serpentine
Crepe
4Z230
$1.98
POST FREE

Hand
Embroidered
Canton Crepe
4Z232
$3.89
POST FREE

Lace Trimmed
Canton Crepe
4Z234
$4.98
POST FREE

Gorgeous robes, kimonos, and negligees , Japanese floral patterns, extravagant hand embroidery, val lace trim, decorative piping, and ornaments.

Shoes, Hats, and Accessories

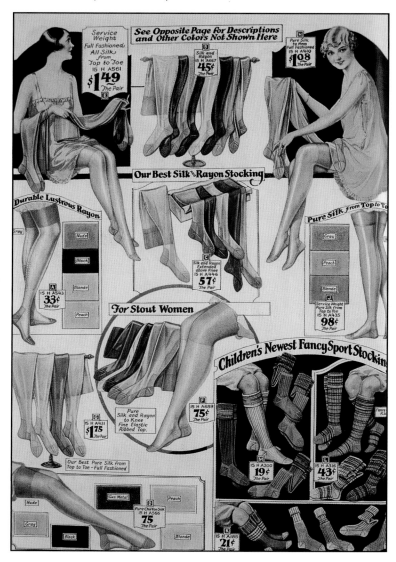

Fully serviceable hosiery, rayon, silk, chiffon, mercerized cotton socks, for women and children.

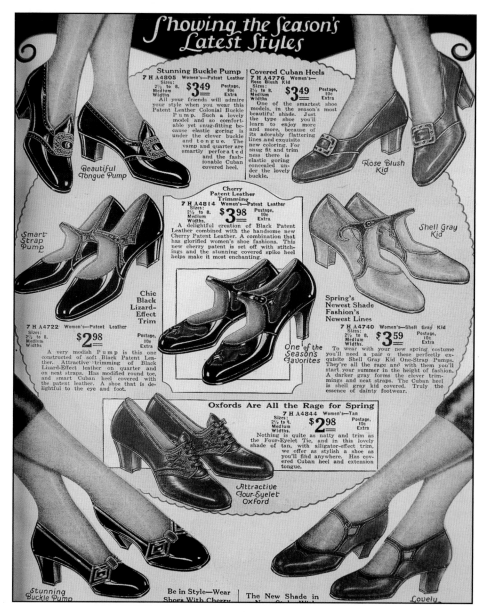

The season's latest styles! Stunning buckle pump, covered Cuban heels, chic black lizard-effect trim, the favorite cherry patent leather trimmed pump, shell gray kid one-strap, stunning buckle pump with cherry patent trim, and of course, Oxfords are all the rage for spring!

The season's sensation! Rose blush or shell gray patent leather. The "Lucille" features a graceful arch and Cuban heel with smart cutouts. Cutouts and a covered Cuban heel add a touch of smartness to the patent leather "Rosamond."

The "Dorothy" shoe, Cuban heel covered with patent leather. Novelty metal buckle enhances the glistening patent leather brilliance.

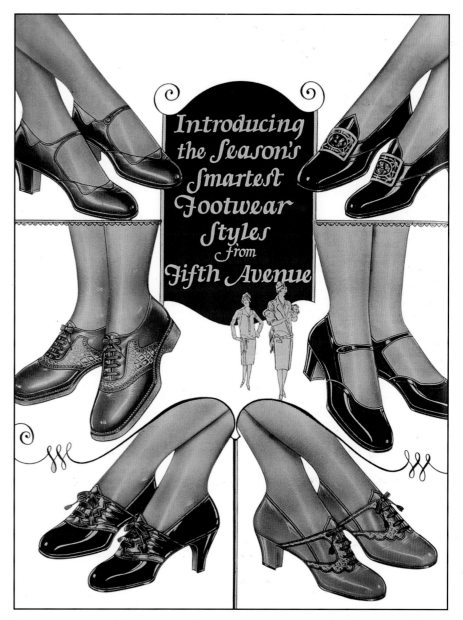

New York's popular styles for footwear. Smart tan-calf eyelet tie with alligator effect leather trimming and covered spike heel, cherry patent leather with contrasting Miami alligator detail. Patent leather tie cut-out oxford, dashing D'Orsay pumps made of soft kid in rose blush or shell gray, glossy black satin pump with one button, two straps, neat stitching and scalloping to prevent any monotony of line. Buckle-front and one-strap patent leather pumps, can be worn with almost any costume.

Strap pump, colonial style spiked heel pump, sport oxford with crepe rubber soul, popular three eyelet tie, and low cut pump five-eyelet oxford. Sturdy and smart styles for the New York summer.

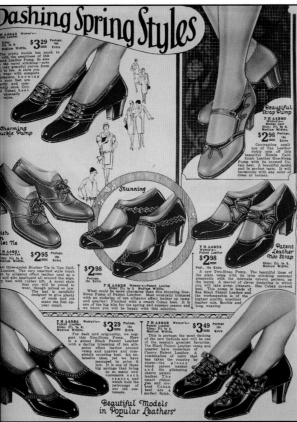

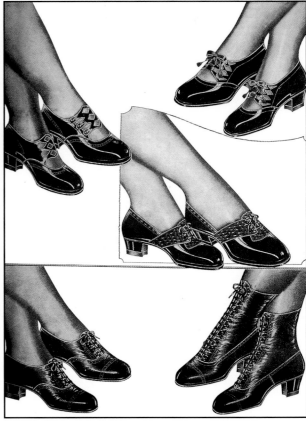

Pumps in patent leather are a sure hit for New York style. Soft kid and black satin are fashionable and fun, with Cuban or spiked heels. Straps, cut outs, and contrasting accents contribute to the trends.

Dashing spring styles! Three-eyelet blucher tie, one or two-strap pumps with contrasting appliqués and accents, patent oxfords in black or cherry, stunning for the lady's foot.

Three button pump or distinctive oxford with charming cut-out designs in black patent leather or black kid, beautiful eyelet tie with black alligator effect leather, oxford tie in brown or black kid for comfort and sturdy support, or perfect boots for extra ankle support with military heel, in dressy kid leather, black or brown.

Oxfords, pumps, comfort slippers in black kid leather, great for walking or at home. Attractive Indian moccasin of soft, comfortable suede-finish leather, with dainty design on vamp. Great for lounging and lazing about.

Restful shoes for tired feet, corrective arch support and abundant comfort with cushion rubber lifts. Low heels equal practicality, while still allowing for a neat, trim style, in black patent or soft black kid leather.

Black patent leather comfort slippers, Opera style, low heel, light and flexible sole. Reliable Juliets, in three attractive patterns – capped toe, plain toe, or with patent leather trim. Guaranteed to be blissfully comfortable. Soft felt moccasins, easy-fitting slippers with stitching on vamp and dainty ribbon trimming, maroon, gray, or blue.

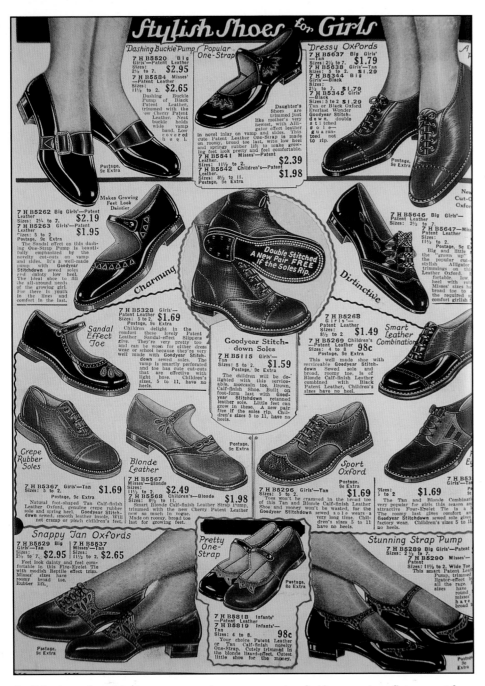

Stylish Shoes for Girls

Dashing Buckle Pump

7 H B5520 Big
Girls'—Patent Leather
Sizes: 2½ to 7.
$2.95
7 H B5584 Misses'
—Patent Leather
Sizes: 11½ to 2.
$2.65

Dashing Buckle
Pump of Black
Patent Leather,
trimmed with the
new Cherry Patent
Leather. Neat
buckle holds
wide vamp
band. Low
covered
heel.

Popular One-Strap

Daughter's
Shoes are
trimmed just
like mother's
newest, with Alli-
gator effect leather
In novel inlay on vamp and sides. This
cute Patent Leather One-Strap is made
on roomy, broad toe last, with low heel
and springy rubber lift to make growing feet look pretty and feel comfortable.
7 H B5541 Misses'—Patent
Leather.
Sizes: 11½ to 2. $2.39
7 H B5542 Children's—Patent
Leather.
Sizes: 8½ to 11. $1.98
Postage, 9c Extra

Dressy Oxfords

7 H B5637 Big Girls'
—Tan
Sizes: 2½ to 7. $1.79
7 H B5638 Girls'—Tan
Sizes: 5 to 2. $1.29
7 H B5344 Big
Girls'—Black
Sizes:
2½ to 7. $1.79
7 H B5345 Girls'
—Black
Sizes: 5 to 2 $1.29
Tan or Black Oxford
Everlast Wonder
Goodyear Stitch-
down, double
stitched
gold-guaran-
teed not
to rip.

7 H B5262 Big Girls'—Patent
Leather
Sizes: 2¼ to 7.
$2.19
7 H B5263 Girls'—Patent
Leather
Sizes: 5 to 2
$1.95
Postage, 9c Extra
The Sandal effect on this dashing One-Strap Pump is beautifully emphasized by the
novelty cut-outs on vamp
and sides. It's a well-made
pump with Goodyear
Stitchdown sewed soles
and dainty low heel.
The ideal shoe to fill
the all-around girl.
For there is youth
in the lines and
comfort in the last.

Makes Growing Feet Look Daintier

Charming

Distinctive

7 H B5646 Big Girls'—
Patent Leather
Sizes: 2½ to 7
$2.95
7 H B5647 Misses'—
Patent Leather
Sizes: 11½ to 2.
Postage, 9c Extra
Big and little
the "grown up"
stylish Alligator
trimmings on the
Leather Oxford,
comfortable, low
heel with rubber.
Misses' sizes on
broad toe to
the required
comfort girlish

*Double Stitched
A New Pair FREE
if the Soles Rip.*

Sandal Effect Toe

7 H B5328 Girls'—
Patent Leather $1.69
Sizes: 5 to 2.
Postage, 9c Extra
Children delight in the
comfort these lovely Patent
Leather Sandal-effect Slippers
give. They're very pretty too
and can be worn for either dress
wear or school because they're very
well made with Goodyear Stitchdown
sewed soles. The
vamp is smartly perforated
and toe has cute cut-outs
that are effective with
light hose. Children's
sizes, 5 to 11, have no
heels.

Goodyear Stitch-down Soles

7 H B5115 Girls'—
Tan
Sizes: 5 to 2. $1.59
Postage, 9c Extra
The children will be de-
lighted with this serviceable, moccasin toe, Brown,
Calf-finish Shoe. Built on
foot-form last with Good-
year Stitchdown retanned
leather sole. Little feet can
grow in these. A new pair
free if the soles rip. Children's sizes 5 to 11, have no
heels.

7 H B526B
Girls'—
Patent Leather
Sizes:
8½ to 2 $1.49
7 H B5269 Children's—
Patent Leather
Sizes: 4 to 8 98c
Postage, 9c Extra
This well made shoe with
serviceable Goodyear Stitch-
down Sewed sole and
broad, roomy toe, is of
Blonde Calf-finish Leather
combined with Black
Patent Leather. Children's
sizes have no heel.

Smart Leather Combination

Crepe Rubber Soles

7 H B5367 Girls'—Tan $1.69
Sizes: 5 to 2.
Postage, 9c Extra
Natural foot-shaped Tan Calf-finish
Leather Oxford, genuine crepe rubber
sole and spring heel. Goodyear Stitch-
down sewed, smooth leather insole. Will
not cramp or pinch children's feet.

Blonde Leather

7 H B5567 Girls'—Blonde
Sizes: 11½ to 2. $2.49
7 H B5568 Children's—Blonde
Sizes: 8½ to 11. $1.98
Smart Blonde Calf-finish Leather Strap Pump,
trimmed with the new Cherry Patent Leather
now in vogue. Made on roomy, broad toe
last for growing feet.

Sport Oxford

7 H B5296 Girls'—Tan $1.69
Sizes: 5 to 2.
Postage, 9c Extra
Toes won't be cramped in the broad toe
of this Tan and Blonde Calf-finish
Shoe and money won't be wasted, for the
Goodyear Stitchdown sewed sole wears a
very long time. Chil-
dren's sizes 5 to 11
have no heels.

Sizes:
5 to 2 $1.69
The Tan and Blonde Combination, very popular for this
season and
attractive Four-Eyelet Tie is a
The roomy last gives comfort and
Goodyear Stitchdown sewed sole gives
satisfactory wear. Children's sizes 5 to 11
no heels.

7 H B53
Girls'—Tan
Postage,
9c E

Snappy Tan Oxfords

7 H B5529 Big
Girls'—Tan
Sizes:
2½ to 7. $2.95
7 H B5537 Misses'—Tan
Sizes:
11½ to 2. $2.65
Feet look dainty and feel comfortable in this Five-Eyelet Tie
with modish Reptile effect trim.
Misses' sizes have
roomy, broad toe.
Rubber lift.

Pretty One-Strap

7 H B5818 Infants'
—Patent Leather
7 H B5819 Infants'—
Tan
Sizes: 4 to 8. 98c
Your choice Patent Leather
or Tan Calf-finish novelty
One-Strap. Cutely trimmed in
the blonde lizard-effect. Cutest
little shoe for the money.

Stunning Strap Pump

7 H B5289 Big Girls'—Patent
Sizes: 2½ to 7.
$1.69
7 H B5290 Misses'—
Patent
Sizes: 11½ to 2. Wide Toe
This smart Patent Leather
Pump, trimmed with
ligator-effect, is
all the rage.
sizes have
round
misses
have
broad

Postage,
9c Extra

Postage,
9c Extra

Stylish shoes for girls. Low pumps, dressy or sport oxfords, one strap flats, great for school, play, or dress. Cut-outs and adorable cherry patent trim accent these girlish styles. Goodyear stitchdown sewed soles on many styles.

Russia Tan Calfskin

Featuring "Miss New York" A new Theo Tie in 2 Popular Colors!

Here's the Greatest Shoe Value in the Country!

Black patent leather or tan Russia calfskin theo pumps, christened "Miss New York," because of the unmistakable chic and charm. Slim cut-out straps across the instep and natty grosgrain ribbon bow matching the leather in color, sturdy flexible leather soles and military rubber heels. Skinner's genuine black satin one strap leather pump, the jaunty silk ribbon side bow is removable.

Smart New York footwear, in patent leather, satin, suede. Dixie tie, black cal finish oxfords, tokio pumps. Cut-out lattice patterns and cheerful bows on select styles add flair. Good wearing flexible leather soles, walking height military heels with rubber top-lift.

Patent leather pump with apricot brown leather back, sunset tan or black calfskin shoe with sunburst perforations, black or gray suede high grade sandal, dressy black suede pump with lustrous black satin inlay, and new "California" sandal with genuine Goodyear welt construction. Guaranteed to last.

Black patent leather or tan Russia calfskin "Miss Hollywood" sandal. Novel perforated vamp in moccasin effect with similar perfs on front strap and quarter, worn with strap under instep or around ankle. Charming "Miss Dixie" style, fetching two-eyelet tie developed in high grade tan Russian calfskin, stylish cut-out perforations across toe and around vamp and quarter. One strap pump of full chrome black patent. Lattice front of genuine black calf leather, modified short vamp, walking height military rubber heels.

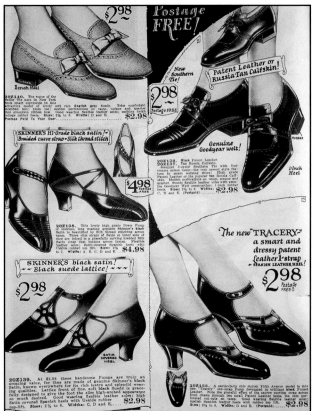

English gray suede sailor ties, black satin braided curved strap pumps, black satin and suede lattice pumps, swagger three-eyelet southern tie with four creases on vamp, and "tracery" leather one-strap pump with Spanish leather heel, each demure and dressy for a fabulous night out on the town.

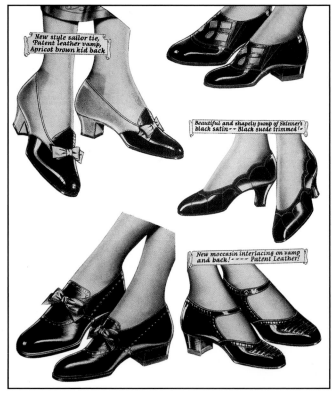

Limousine brand shoes, highest grade in smartest New York styles. One-eyelet sailor tie, English kid gore pump, radio sandal, patent side lace bow sandal, black velvet evening slippers, selected styles with Uskide top lift to double the wear of heels.

A favorite of Fifth Avenue… chic one-eyelet sailor tie with vamp of finest quality black patent and back of rich apricot brown kid, silk ribbon bow to match. Fashionable gore pump in brilliant black patent has smartly designed lattice front. Handsome sailor ties fashioned of black or brown Vici kid, stylish perforations on vamp, tongue, and quarter. Rich material and graceful lines characterize a beautiful black satin and suede pump. Novel moccasin effect interlacing decorates the vamp, collar, and quarter of a striking one-strap glossy black patent pump.

88

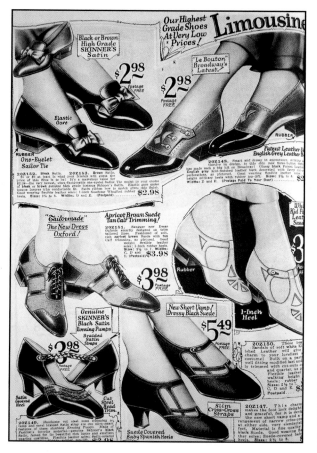

Limousine brand shoes, New York's finest styles in black, brown, apricot, great for evening wear or when you want to dress to feel your best. Pumps, oxfords, and sandals, for the matronly dame.

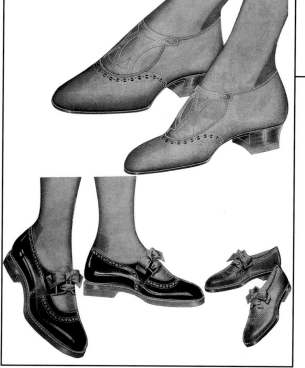

Lovely evening slippers of rich sparkling genuine silver or gold brocade, one strap model built on slim, graceful heel. Braided strap spring dress shoe of glossy black patent leather, fancy stitching on vamp and quarter adds charm. Brilliant black patent leather low heel shoe with plain toe that contrasts strikingly with the dressy cut out strap and quarter with modish perforation on vamp. Flexible for added comfort.

Attractive shoe with cut-out lattice front, buttoning on either side, plain toe and modishly perforated vamp, sturdy rubber heel, all nut-brown calf-finish leather, gray suede with gray leather lattice, black suede with black patent lattice, black velvet with black patent lattice, and black patent with tan leather lattice, patent leather with smoked elk tongue, for sport or dress wear, two-eyelet tie with stylish perforated cutouts on vamp and quarter and silk ribbon laces,

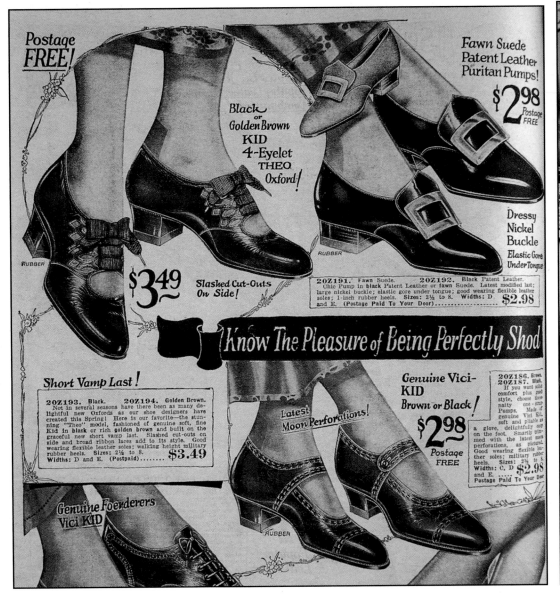

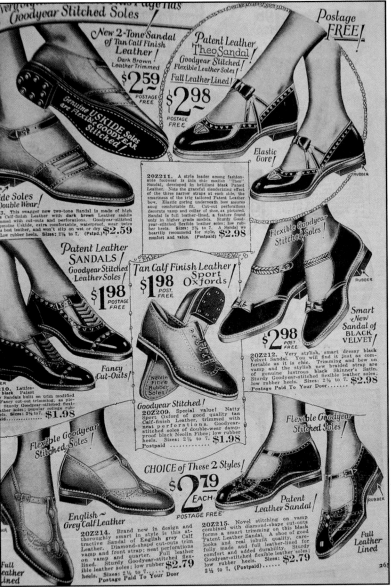

Theo oxfords, Puritan pumps, and novelty moon perforated one strap pumps in black patent, brown or black vici kid, or golden brown kid. Your feet have never been so stylish!

Patent leather sandals and oxfords, made on the finest welts. Sturdy Goodyear-stitched flexible leather soles, low rubber heels.

Strong, solid shoes to get you around town! Comfort styled, attractive and modish.

Fashion's favorite styles. Oxfords, buckle pumps, chic strap pumps, decorated with contrasting leather effects and trimming. Comfortable and sturdy.

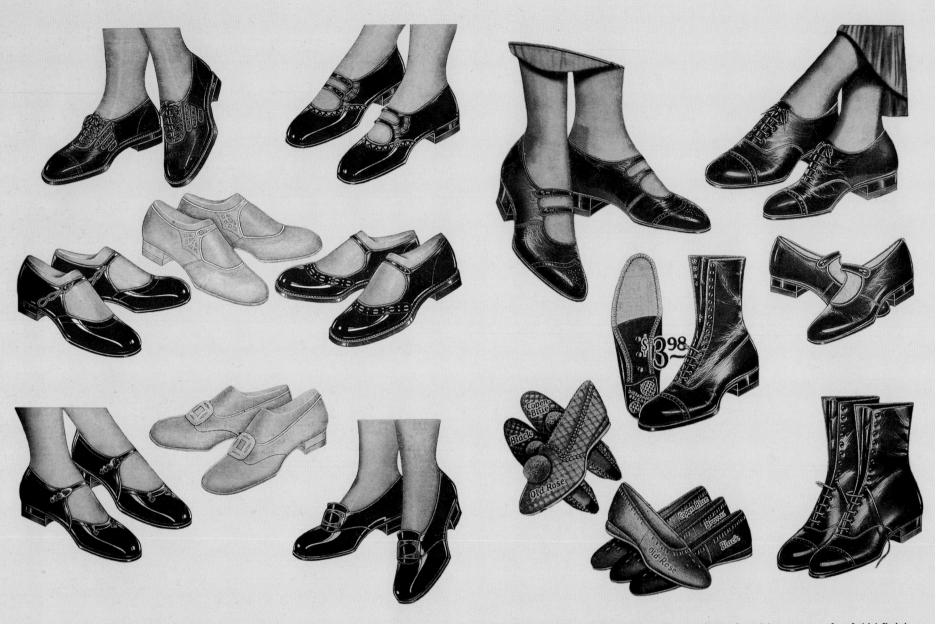

Just like mom, sport the latest fashions for feet.

Kid finish leather cushion inner sole, very comfortable pumps of soft kid-finish leather, plain toe. Good wearing flexible soles.

Athletic shoes for sport, women's storm rubbers, cross strap pumps for casual wear and play. Palm Beach moccasin bluchers, and soft and comfortable black boudoir slippers with hand-turned flexible leather soles.

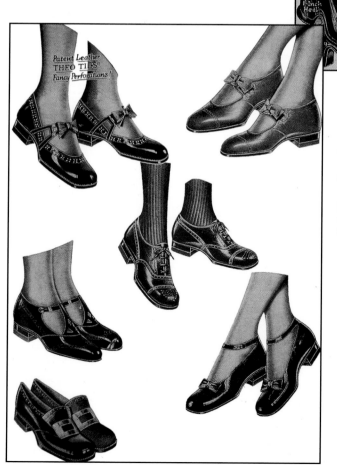

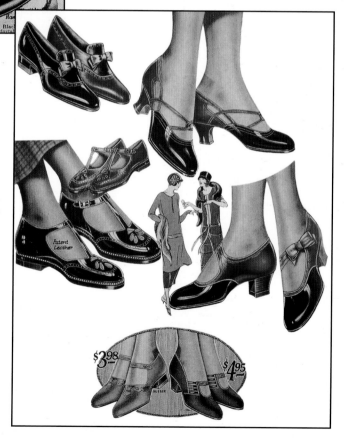

Dashing "Theo" tie of black patent leather with swagger cut-out strap and neat ribbon bow or Russian tan calf finish. Radio sandal with smart cutouts, dressy in glossy black patent. Puritan pumps in gray suede or black patent, pretty nickel buckle. 1925 edition of "Mary Jane" for women and children, a most popular and classic style, in black patent.

Slave strap pump, sailor ties, Miss Hollywood sandal with unique cut-outs and perforations, and 2-tone patent leather-blonde kid with chic bow above vamp.

6Z801

$2 39 Postage FREE

6Z80? $3 88 Postage FREE

6Z801. Worthy of this prominent place at the beginning of our Millinery Section is this youthful, becoming Poke Shape. It is made of All-Over Straw—a favorite material for the new millinery. The brim is about 2½ ins. wide in the front and very narrow in the back. It is faced with Poplin and there is a large bow of Poplin at the back, which gives the Hat a slightly larger effect. Hand Embroidery in Metallic and Silk Thread forms a novel design on the front. Colors: Titian (new shade of golden rust), powder blue or black. This is a very beautiful hat and a remarkably big value at our price................$2.39
Postage Paid To Your Door

Ostrich feathers, decorative flowers, and poplin bows accentuate New York's finest millinery!

6Z895 $3 97 POST FREE

6Z896 $2 19 POST FREE

6Z898 $1 65 POST FREE

Advanced New York styles, made from the finest materials. Felt, faille taffeta, and Milan hemp, Silk Swiss hair braid. Silk and Satin trimmings, rhinestones, flowers, ribbons, and streamers. Very becoming for spring. Rose, Copen, Pablo, Gobolin, black, green, sand, coral, Navy, red.

Short back silk plaited Georgette hat with feather pompom gives effective touch of Paris. Dress hat with dented mushroom brim, all over silk straw, wide fold of lustrous silk taffeta around crown, with clusters of red cherries to trim.

16 H 817 $2 98

16 H 823 $1 98

16 H 813 $2 49

16 H 813A Headsize, about 22½ inches. OUR PRICE, Each..............$2.49 Postage 22c Extra COLORS: Rose, Copen, Gooseberry (Green) or Orchid, State Color. Row upon row of accordion pleated ribbon forms the crown of this pretty poke and on the brim dainty Val lace alternates with the ribbon. Dainty trimming of silk plush flowers. Val lace and silk floss embroidery. The brim is faced with self color taffeta.

16 H 811 $2 79

16 H 815 $1 79

16 H 811A Headsize, about 22½ inches. OUR PRICE

94

16 H 833 $1.98

16 H 841 $3.49

16 H 843 $1.98

16 H 833A Headsize, about 22½ inches.
PRICE, Each... $1.98 Postage, 12c Extra
COLORS: Black and Rose, Green or Sand, Gobelin and Gray, or Oak and Sand.
The crown of this lovely Hat is made of a fine quality Proxyline Hair Braid and the poke brim faced with taffeta and shirred around the edge of the brim. Large silk flower and foliage on the side.

16 H 829 $1.98

16 H 839 $2.98

16 H 831 $2.98

16 H 839A Headsize, abt. 22½ ins.
OUR PRICE, Each... $2.98 Postage, 12c Extra
COLORS: Shell Pink, White, Copen or French Beige. State Color.
A typical party Hat of All Silk Satin and Sheer Georgette brim, edged with self-color Visca straw braid. The crown is finished with satin ribbon band and a streamer at the side. A rosebud and foliage adds a touch of color. A very pretty hat and an exceptional value.

16 H 835 $5.98

16 H 827 $3.98

16 H 835A Headsize, abt. 22½ ins.
OUR PRICE, Each... $5.98 Postage, 12c Extra
COLORS: Mother Goose (Tan), Black, Gooseberry or Gobelin Blue, all with brilliant Rainbow facings. State Color.
This Hat is even prettier in reality than in the picture because only then can you see the beautiful quality. The fine Swiss crown has a wide brim of Faille Taffeta. Draped crepe de chine band around crown. Velvet ribbon bow in front and again as trimming on top of brim.

16 H 837 $4.98

Wide brims with flashy bows will catch any eye, or a close-fitting hat will flatter and impress. Black, Castillian red, gooseberry, Gobolin blue, mother goose (tan), Pablo, conch shell.

16 H 849 $3.29

16 H 847 $3.98

16 H 855 $3.29

Excellent quality silk Swiss hair braid fashions a smart picture hat. Brim of all silk crepe de chine with a flange of changeable taffeta ribbon and plush flowers. Taffeta-faced brimmed picture hat with short back, two large plush poppies in harmonizing colors make up the sectional crown. Close-fitting hat with crown of fine Swiss hair, prettily trimmed with a novelty metallic silk ribbon rose and silk plush foliage.

16 H 845 $4.98

16 H 851 $3.49

16 H 857 $2.98

16 H 853 $1.98

Azure accents, embroidered crepe, silk rosettes, velvet ribbon loops, and silk braids adorn the most stylish New York hats.

95

Beautiful tam effect all silk faille taffeta is combined with the new crochet straw. Heavy silk tassel drawn through a crescent-shaped ornament on the side, black, castillian red, sand and wild honey, or Copen blue. Picture hat with good quality all silk taffeta crown and finished with a band of grosgrain ribbon, large silk rose for effect. Copen, black, green, Pablo.

Semi-high crown on a close fitting all silk faille taffeta hat is accentuated by rows of tubular stitching and contrasting color braid. Perfectly adorable picture hat with proxyline braid crown and wide transparent brim, Swiss hair flange and grosgrain ribbon embroidered in silk adds finishing touch. Pablo, gooseberry, Copen, black, Gobelin blue.

Youthful, attractive hats for incredibly chic young women. All silk faille, straw braid, and taffeta make for extraordinary summer wear.

Smart, close-fitting styles for the matronly woman. For a higher fashion look, a wide brimmed model with wide satin ribbon and pleated fancy on the side. And for the sporty woman in each of us, the Vagabond sailor style, made of lightweight azure braid with a new indented crown, and roman-striped ribbon finished with a flat bow and feather at the side.

Make your millinery collection complete with a gorgeous picture hat with embroidery or plush foliage effect. Turn heads everywhere you go with these close-fitting styles, or wide brimmed models.

16 H 929
$3.98

16 H 915
$3.98

16 H 925
$1.49

16 H 921
$3.29

16 H 929A Headsize, about 22 ins.
OUR PRICE,
Each.................. $3.98 Postage,
12c Extra
COLORS: Pablo and Copen; Tiger Lily;
Oak and Pablo; or Gooseberry Green.
The high tam crown of Brocaded Paisley Silk has a draped taffeta band. The smart ripple brim is trimmed with straw braid and cluster of silk and gilt flowers.

16 H 915A Headsize, about 22½ ins.
OUR PRICE,
Each.................. $3.98 Postage,
12c Extra
COLORS: Pablo, Conch Shell, Gobelin Blue or Gooseberry Green. State Color.
This new Off-the-Face Hat, with its stylish high crown of fine quality Crochet Straw Braid, is combined with All Silk Taffeta. The tubular stitching is very new. Draped taffeta band and bow at side.

16 H 925A Headsize, about 22½ ins.
OUR PRICE,
Each.................. $1.49 Postage,
12c Extra
COLORS: Black, Oak, Red or Gooseberry Green. State Color.
Every woman needs an inexpensive hat for every day. This one is made of a good quality Peanut Straw, trimmed with a Roman-stripe ribbon bow and novelty buckle in the front.

16 H 921A Headsize, about 22½ ins.
OUR PRICE,
Each.................. $3.29 Post...
COLORS: Rose, Green, Pablo or B...
Another very smart Hat w... fits close to the head. Fashio... of All Silk Taffeta with a s... transparent brim of Swiss silk... braid. Tubular stitching on... crown, and trimmed with two g... grain ribbon fancies.

16 H 927
$1.98

16 H 923
$3.49

16 H 93...
$1.79

16 H 923A Headsize, PRICE,
about 23 inches. Each.......... $3.49 Postage,
12c Extra
COLORS: Black, Oakwood, Jungle Green or Henna. State Color.
The crown of this pretty Dress Hat is creased in sections and the brim is of rich looking floral metallic cloth. There is a wreath of silk flowers and berries across the front. The broad, brocaded brim is faced with a quality taffeta. A very becoming model and very reasonable for such quality and style.

16 H 927A Headsize, PRICE,
about 22½ inches. Each.......... $1.98 Postage,
12c Extra
COLORS: Green, Light Oakwood, Black and Rose or Gobelin Blue. State Color.
One could tell at a glance that this Hat of All Silk Taffeta was created in New York. The sectional crown is trimmed with an insert of straw braid which also finishes the wide taffeta brim. Large silk rose on the side and grosgrain ribbon band.

15 H 935A Headsize, PRICE,
about 23 inches. Each.......... $1.79
COLORS: Black, Monkeyskin, Jungle Green or...
A most unusual value that must be see... appreciated. The crown of this pliable Straw Hat is smartly creased and trimm... hand embroidered stitching and a large s... The wide brim is bound with grosgrain an... up in the back. The band is also of gr... The colors are lovely.

16 H 933
$2.98

16 H 931
$2.98

16 H 919
$1.98

16 H...
$4.

16 H 933A Headsize, abt. 21½ ins.
OUR PRICE,
Each.......... $2.98 Postage,
12c Extra
COLORS: Castilian Red, Gooseberry Green, Pablo or Gobelin Blue. State Color.
The crown...

16 H 931A Headsize, abt. 22½ ins.
OUR PRICE,
Each.......... $2.98 Postage,
12c Extra
COLORS: Castilian Red, Copen, Oakwood or Black. State Color.
Heavy All Silk Bengaline Rib...

16 H 919A Headsize, abt. 22½ ins.
OUR PRICE,
Each.......... $1.98 Postage,
12c Extra
COLORS: Black and Crabapple; Red and Navy; Oak and Pablo, or Green.
We doubt whether you coul...

16 H 917A Headsize...
OUR PRICE,
Each.......... $1.95...

16 H 913
$3.29

16 H 897
$1.98

16 H 901
$2.98

16 H 907
$5.98

16 H 91
$2.38

16 H 911A Headsize, about...
OUR PRICE,
Each.......... $2.39 Postage, 12c Ext...

16 H 901A Headsize, about...
inches.
OUR PRICE, $2.98 Postage.

Styles that charm… brocaded paisley silk with draped taffeta, off-the-face hat with stylish high crown of fine crochet straw braid, peanut straw, felt, all silk taffeta, floral metallic broadcloth, all silk bengaline decorations.

16 H 955
$1⁹⁸

16 H 949
$1⁴⁹

16 H 957
$3²⁹

16 H 953
98¢

16 H 947
$1⁷⁹

16 H 951
$2⁹⁸

16 H 951A Headsize, Shell Pink, Copen, Pablo or Gooseberry. $2.98 Postage, about 22½ inches 12c Extra
The sectional crown of this lovely Picture Hat is fashioned of a fine quality Silk Bengaline and the wide transparent brim is of a fine quality hair braid. Bengaline ribbon band and beautiful silk flowers and foliage on the front.

16 H 943
$1⁶⁹

16 H 941
$2⁴⁹

16 H 945
$2¹⁹

16 H 937
$1⁷⁹

16 H 939
$3⁹⁸

16 H 941A Headsize, abt. 22½ ins. Postage, OUR PRICE. 12c Extra
Each, $2.49
COLORS: Green, Black, Red or Pablo. This very chic Hat has a high crown of a fine quality All Silk

16 H 939A Headsize, about 22¼ ins. Postage, OUR PRICE. 12c Extra
Each, $3.98
COLORS: Black, Oakwood, Royal Blue or

16 H 989
$1⁹⁸

16 H 981
$2³⁹

16 H 981A Headsize, OUR PRICE, $2.39 Postage, about 23 inches Each, 12c Extra
COLORS: Gobelin Blue and Gray; Black and Red; Oakwood and Sand; or Gooseberry Green. State Choice.
One of the prettiest Hats of the season. Good quality two-color Patent Milan with a colorful wreath of buttercups, poppies and daisies. There is a grosgrain ribbon band around the crown. The broad brim has the popular short-back.

16 H 979
$1⁹⁸

16 H 985
$2⁹⁸

16 H 987
$3⁴⁹

16 H 977
$1⁹⁵

Youthful poke of fine quality Visca all-over braid, taffeta faced brim trimmed with large silk rose and foliage on the side. Good quality two-color patent Milan with a colorful wreath of buttercups, poppies, and daisies.

Try something new this spring… smart models for sport or dress wear. Straw is lightweight for summer and offers versatility and pliability. Wide brims to protect sensitive eyes from bright sun, and close fitting styles for a becoming night out on the town. Ornaments add final effect, including rhinestone pins, bows, ribbons, and ostrich feather bands.

Simple hats can be trimmed with bows, ribbons,
pins, and silk flowers for stunning effect.

Fashionable, close-fitting hats, trimmed with wreathes of fruit, silk pastel chrysan-
themums, Aigrette all over straw, or grosgrain ribbon bows to add the perfect
touch.

Refreshingly different styles, close-fitting dress hats, modeled after the very latest from Paris, high crown styles with exotic adornments.

Poke bonnet in lustrous satin, all over straw and taffeta blend, Milan straw, dressy baronette haircloth turban, and metallic cloth with taffeta bands with mushroom brim.

High crown models are in style this season, and don't forget your trimmings! Popular colors include tan, powder blue, cranberry red, black, golden rust, and cocoa.

Graceful lines, smart trimmings. Rich looking styles in the latest styles: draped turbans, mushroom brim, and chic turned-up brims. All feature elaborate trims of ostrich feathers, satin ribbon fringe, flowers, fruit, and silk floss stitching.

Mushroom or rolled brim hats offer charming style for the young lady. Trimmings include ostrich flues, grosgrain ribbon, pastel fruit and flowers, and novel side ornaments.

Becoming hats for young girls – just like mothers!

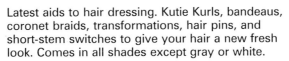

Becoming hats for young women, short back styles just like the grown-ups. Each adorned with a fashionable effect.

Latest aids to hair dressing. Kutie Kurls, bandeaus, coronet braids, transformations, hair pins, and short-stem switches to give your hair a new fresh look. Comes in all shades except gray or white.

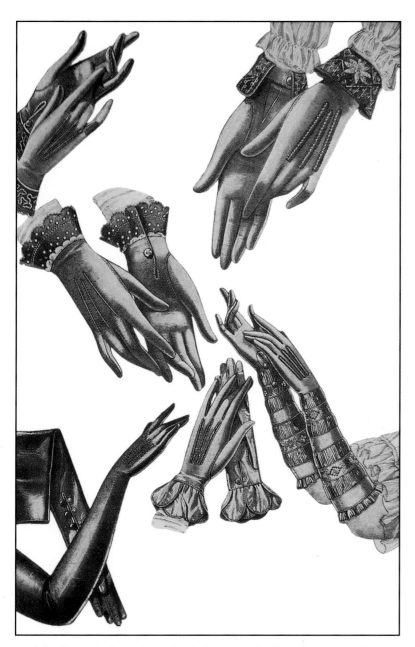

Stylish gloves in French top lambskin, novelty French top kid glove, glace lambskin, Milanese silk, and glace kid with Paris point embroidery accents and scalloped edges for effect. Brown, beaver, black, white, tan, or gray.

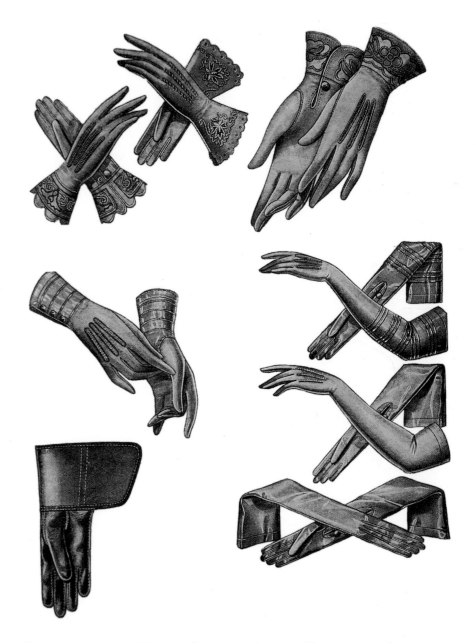

Chamoisuede embroidered cuff gauntlet gloves, folding gauntlet of heavy lambskin, or long length heavy quality Milanese silk gloves with arm tucked to give the new, smart bracelet effect. Extra durable double finger tipped heavy silk gloves in popular 16-button length.

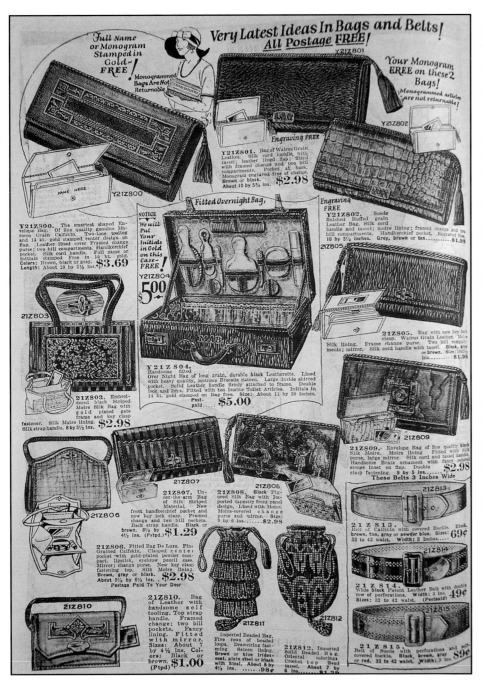

What better to complete an outfit than a stylish necklace! Pearls, simulated rubies, sapphires, emeralds, and topaz, one, two, or three strands. Round and oval decorative bead strands of plated nickel, sterling silver, and Platinoid-finish.

Handsome bags and belts for the debonair lady.
Beaded, embroidered styles, leather.

Men's Fashions

Day Wear

Hand tailored suit, "Prince of Wales" all wool cassimere model, two-button, single-breasted sack coat, extra wide straight trousers cut on approved English lines, brown or horizon blue. Dress shirt of fine quality lustrous imported English broadcloth, powder blue, white, or tan. English Sateen dress shirt, attached collar, faced sleeves, coat style. All wool Overplaid LaPorte suit, single-breasted coat, three quarter belt, plaits in back and front.

All wool worsted for conservative dressers, woven with pleasingly, inconspicuous broken silk stripes, three button single breasted coat, flap covered side pockets. Black, medium gray, brown. All wool cassimere in modern diamond weave, three button single breasted style coat, semi-peaked long roll lapels, collarless style vest, popular medium width pants, straight or cuff bottoms, gray or brown. All wool worsted suit with two pairs of trousers in neat, harmonizing striped pattern, brown, steel gray, Navy blue.

All virgin wool worsted suit, tailored and modeled to the forms of living men for a perfect fit. Double sewn seams for harder wear. Three button conservative style coat, five button vest, medium width trousers with straight or cuff bottoms. Navy blue, oxford gray, dark brown.

Dressy marvlo serge suit, three button young men's model with three patch pockets, regular five button model vest, stylish two button wide waistband trousers, wide belt loops, straight or cuff bottoms. Dark Navy. Marvlo serge suit or all wool worsted blue suit with snappy silver stripe, stylishly tailored in three-button, double breasted styles, full cut trousers with straight or cuff bottoms.

Serge suits in single-or double-breasted styles, collarless vests and straight or cuff bottom trousers to complement. Navy blue, gray, or dark brown.

Cool summer suits, in gabardine, genuine linen, Palm Beach cloth styles. Light weight and comfortable, two or three button conservative coats. Navy, black, gray, tan, brown.

All wool cassimere, soft and fine, single breasted coat with long roll lapels, English cut vest with straight bottom, extra wide Prince of Wales trousers with plain or cuff bottoms. Brown or horizon blue (blue-gray). All wool imported suiting loomed in England, double breasted swagger coat, hand tailored throughout so as not to lose shape. London lavender-gray, or brown.

Men's and young men's well tailored, double-service suits. All wool worsted serge, dependable all 'round service and good appearance.

Suit of washable Daytona suiting, looks cool and smart through the hot weather. Single-breasted sack coat, tailored with patch pockets and broad French facing, tan stripe or gray stripe. Spring model of genuine Palm Beach cloth, guarantees serviceability. No vest. Gray, brown, or blue, with neat stripe.

Smart all wool cassimere, all wool worsted serge, and all wool flannel sport models! A necessity in the wardrobe of every well dressed young man! Horizon blue, medium brown, gray.

Here Is the **STYLISH SUIT** Shown On The **FRONT COVER**

Extra Trousers

English Style

Hand Tailored

High Grade All Wool Worsted Serge, 50Z441

with 2 Pairs of Trousers 50Z440 $21.95 POST FREE

Grey All Wool Flannel Extra Trousers 49Z116 $5.95 POST FREE

On the Front Cover We Show these Grey Trousers Worn with the Serge Coat and Vest of Suit Pictured Above $21.50 POST FREE

Hand Tailored

Extra Trousers

New Spring Sport Model

Conservative

All Wool Suiting Model 50Z43 $13.9 POST FREE

Cravenette Processed REG. U.S. PAT. OFF.

Cravenetted Worsted Gabardine 52Z400 $16.85 POST FREE

Khaki Drill Two Piece Suit 49Z101 $5.98 POST FREE

Men's well built sturdy outing clothes. Water-proof collegiate slicker and cravenetted coat! Worsted gabardine double service coat. Olive drab moleskin, khaki drill two piece suits, or smart yellow oiled slicker, superb for the man who is outdoors a lot for sport or work.

All wool cassimere two trouser suit with conservative lines, two-button, single-breasted sack coat, pronounced English style, horizon blue or medium brown. Dressy, well tailored business suit cut on trim lines, made of sturdy, high grade firmly woven material, three button single breasted sack, brown or gray with neat subdued pattern. Sport suit with snappy, swagger features, tailored throughout in A-1 manner, brown or horizon blue.

Conservative cut all wool Navy blue worsted, snappy new all wool tweed sports style, or New York model all wool cassimere suits for men and young men. Lined throughout with durable, lustrous satin-finish Venetian, or strong all wool alpaca. Gray, brown, Navy blue, horizon blue.

Styles here to suit the man of conservative taste, or the younger man who wants snappy lines! Virgin all wool worsted serge or striped all wool worsted suits, single or double breasted. All wool flannel jazz suit with smart lines, three button front closing, and semi-peak lapels. Brown, Navy blue, horizon blue.

Dressy all wool cassimere trousers, blended indistinct pencil stripe, well cut and tailored, stoutly stitched. Brown or horizon blue. English cut, fine quality gray all wool flannel trousers for dress, sport, or evening wear.

109

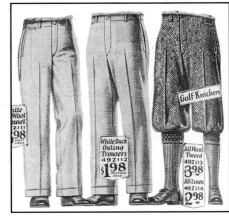

Dress trousers and knickers, for any occasion, in the sturdiest materials for the best value. All wool white flannel, white duck outing trousers, striped all wool worsted, wool mixed serge, and all wool worsted herringbone stripe. Brown, navy blue, black, white, tan, gray.

Dress trousers for men and young men, all wool cassimere, all wool serge, neat striped cassimere. Medium gray, brown, blue gray, or dark Navy.

Full cut and well made dress shirts, silky quality mercerized pongee, satin striped Habutai, or corded madras materials, French cuffs and laundered neckband. Tan, gray, blue, white, solid ground with assorted stripes.

Handsome dress shirts of satin striped, English broadcloth, brilliant fibre silk stripes, and all silk crepe de Chine in white, multicolored stripes, tan, or blue. These shirts can be laundered again and again without losing their original soft and silky quality!

Imported all silk pongee, shantung, and corded madras shirts to impress New York's debutantes. Coat style with attached collar, breast pocket, and band cuffs. Natural tan, white, blue, and white ground with assorted stripes.

Attractive and breezy dress shirts made full and beautifully finished. Madras, Soisette, and English broadcloth, smooth and comfortable for summer wear.

111

Summer sports shirts, cool elbow length sleeves, double yoke, breast pocket. Khaki, white, tan, blue chambray.

85¢ Each

Neckband Style

Striped or Checked Patterns

Fine dress shirt, smartest percale patterned shirting, neckband style with French cuffs, or attached collar.

Mercerized broadcloth shirt, attached collar, center pleat, faced sleeves, and soft buttoned cuffs, trimmed with ocean pearl buttons. White, tan, blue.

Sturdy men's shirts, sweaters, and blazer jackets, for sports or general wear. Neckband or attached collar
styles, in blues, tans, whites, and colorful patterns, plaids, checks, and stripes, for all the summer rage.

Swagger sports sweaters for the golf course, the home, or the office. Classy up-to-date attire for sporty men. Black, brown, Navy blue, maroon, buff, beaver, poudre blue, or royal.

Golf knickers and collegian wide bottom dress trousers, all wool striped flannel, woven knickers in Scotch weave cheviot or all wool overplaid flannel, and handsome all wool cassimere.

For men who give their clothes hard service, sturdy moleskin breeches, trousers, and work pants are comfortable and good looking. Brown and drab moleskin, gray herringbone stripe, and khaki.

Our Best
All Wool
Striped
Flannel
4 H A2724
$4.98

All Wool
Knickers
in the
Latest
Weaves
4 H A2761
$4.25

Handsome
All Wool
Cassimere
in the
Newest
Colors
4 H A2751
$3.98

$3.49

$1.39
Pair

Double Front
Blue Denim
Overall Pants
$1.19

$1.49
Heavy
Khaki

State
Waist
and
Inseam
Measure
When
Ordering

Dark
Oxford
Gray
Whipcord
45 H 253

Our Boys
Breeches
are Shown
on Page
197b

High
Grade
Brown
Moleskin
Breeches
45 H 234
$2.59

Grau Striped
Worsted
45 H 346

Heavy outdoor work requires a heavy duty overall pant, with double knee and double front. Made of heavy weight indigo denim; all seams triple-lock stitched. Comfortable and good-looking heavy khaki breeches provide ease of movement and more real enjoyment of the outdoors.

For long, dependable service, gray striped cottonade work pants, or gray striped cotton worsted trousers with usual pockets and fittings.

Six big features about the indigo blue denim jumper: double front, double seat, pre-shrunk fast color heavy weight denim, whip stitched button holes, two-seam triple sewn legs, and non rust buttons. Excellent for the hard working man.

Made For Hard Wear Gray Striped Cottonade 49Z139 $1.49 POST.FREE

Striped Cotton Worsted 49Z140 $1.98 POST.FREE

Pieces Sold Separately

$5.98

Waterproof Windproof Featherweight

Duck hunting outfit, olive drab coat, cap, and trousers. Comfortable windbreaker carefully made of water-proof balloon cloth, comfortable yet light in weight. Large collar, flap protected pockets.

Jacket
49 Z 145
$1.00
POSTAGE FREE

Jacket
49 Z 147
$1.49
POSTAGE FREE

Triple Stitched
Heavy Weight
Stifel Drill

Overalls
49 Z 146
$1.00
POSTAGE FREE

Heavy Weight
Indigo Blue
Denim
Triple Stitched

DOUBLE FRONT
AND KNEES

Overalls
49 Z 148
$1.49
POSTAGE FREE

A Big Favorite
Triple Stitched
Strong Khaki Drill
Overall Suit

49 Z 151
$1.98
POSTAGE FREE

Denim overalls, stifle drill worksuits with jackets, triple stitched strong khaki drill suits, for superior service and durability. Double front knees, reinforced seams and pockets. Indigo blue, khaki, blue, and white.

Great for Wear!

15 Z 900
89¢
POST. FREE

Yarn Dyed Chambray
15 Z 901
2 FOR 98¢
POST. FREE

Fast Color
Full Sizes

15 Z 902
98¢
POST. FREE

Extra Full Cut

15 Z 903
89¢
POST. FREE

15 Z 904
$1.39
POST. FREE

15 Z 905
79¢
POST. FREE

Big, strong, husky work shirts in khaki service cloth, yarn dyed chambray, golden rule chambray, genuine stifle cloth, mercerized khaki jean, and fine yarn smooth and durable chambray. All high grade, button front, doubled stitched and double yoke styles.

Good looking flat knit all wool sports sweater is warm but not bulky and can be worn under a coat on chilly days or indoors. Coat style with v-neck, brown heather, or plain buff. Half cardigan rib stitch with rack stitch around bottom and on pocket tops. Brown, Navy blue, maroon. Smart, dressy cricket neck pullover knit of soft, high grade all wool yarns, two color stripe trimming on neck, cuffs, and around bottom. White, gray, or buff with contrasting stripes.

Heavy quality Rayon fibre silk ties in novelty stripes and patterns. Good looking shirt of smooth and silky English broadcloth, separate collar of self material, laundered neckband, French cuffs. Tan, blue, or white.

118

Topcoats for rain or shine.

Waterproof oiled slickers and rubber clothing. Young men's collegian slicker, firemen's black rubber coat, police or "watchmen's" black rubber coat.

Shoes, Hats, and Accessories

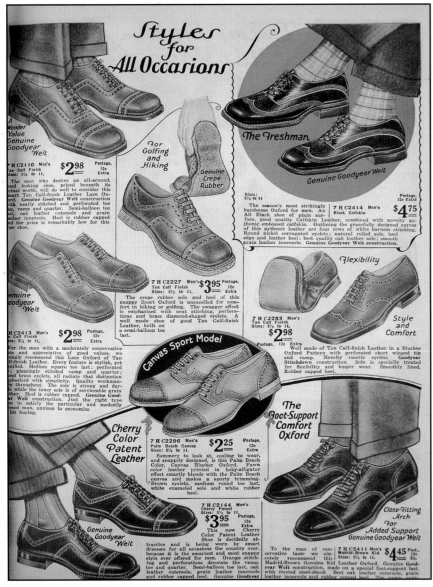

Styles for All Occasions

Wonder Value Genuine Goodyear Welt

7 H C2110 Men's
Tan Calf Finish
Sizes: 5½ to 11.
$2.98
Postage, 12c Extra

The man who desires an all-around, good looking shoe, priced beneath its actual worth, will do well to consider this smart Tan Calf-finish Leather Lace Oxford. Genuine Goodyear Welt construction with neatly stitched and perforated toe cap, vamp and quarter. Semi-balloon toe last, oak leather outersole and grain leather innersole. Heel is rubber capped and the price is remarkably low for this type shoe.

For Golfing and Hiking

Genuine Crepe Rubber

7 H C2227 Men's
Tan Calf Finish
Sizes: 5½ to 11.
$3.95
Postage 12c Extra

The crepe rubber sole and heel of this snappy Sport Oxford is unexcelled for comfort in hiking or golfing. The swagger effect is emphasized with neat stitching, perforations and brass diamond-shaped eyelets. A well made shoe of good Tan Calf-finish Leather, built on a semi-balloon toe last.

The Freshman

Genuine Goodyear Welt

7 H C2414 Men's
Black Calfskin
Sizes: 5½ to 11
$4.75
Postage, 12c Extra

The season's most strikingly handsome Oxford for men. An All Black shoe of plain surface, good quality Calfskin Leather, combined with novelty pythonic embossed calfskin. Outlining the gracefully designed curves of this pythonic leather are four rows of white harness stitching. Round nickel corrugated eyelets; natural rolled sole, heel edge and leather heel; best quality oak leather sole; smooth grain leather innersole. Genuine Goodyear Welt construction.

Flexibility — Style and Comfort

7 H C2253 Men's
Tan Calf Finish
Sizes: 5½ to 11.
$2.98
Postage, 12c Extra

Well made of Tan Calf-finish Leather in a Blucher Oxford Pattern with perforated short winged tip and vamp. Novelty rosette eyelets, Goodyear Stitchdown construction. Sole is specially treated for flexibility and longer wear. Smoothly lined. Rubber capped heel.

Genuine Goodyear Welt

7 H C2413 Men's
Calf Finish
Sizes: 5½ to 11.
$2.98
Postage, 12c Extra

For the man with a moderately conservative taste and appreciative of good values, we strongly recommend this Lace Oxford of Tan Calf-finish Leather. Every feature is stylish, yet dignified. Medium square toe last; perforated and pleasingly stitched vamp and quarter; and brass eyelets, all radiate that distinction emphasized with simplicity. Quality workmanship throughout. The sole is strong and durable while the inner sole is of serviceable grain leather. Heel is rubber capped. Genuine Goodyear Welt construction. Just the right type shoe to satisfy the particular and modestly dressed man, anxious to economize on his buying.

Canvas Sport Model — Cherry Color Patent Leather

7 H C2296 Men's
Palm Beach Canvas
Sizes: 5½ to 11.
$2.25
Postage, 12c Extra

Summery to look at, cooling to wear, and snappily designed, is this Palm Beach Color, Canvas Blucher Oxford. Fawn color leather printed in baby-alligator effect smartly blends with the Palm Beach canvas and makes a sporty trimming. Brown eyelets, medium round toe last, white enameled sole and white rubber heel.

7 H C2144 Men's
Cherry Patent
Sizes: 5½ to 11.
$3.95
Postage, 12c Extra

This new Cherry Color Patent Leather Shoe is decidedly attractive and is being worn by smart dressers for all occasions the country over, because it is the smartest and most snappy style ever offered for men. Orange stitching and perforations decorate the vamp, toe and quarter. Semi-balloon toe last, oak leather outersole, grain leather innersole and rubber capped heel. Genuine Goodyear Welt.

The Foot-Support Comfort Oxford

Close-Fitting Arch For Added Support Genuine Goodyear Welt

7 H C2411 Men's
Madrid-Brown Kid
Sizes: 5½ to 11.
$4.45
Post. 12c Ex.

To the man of conservative taste we sincerely recommend this Madrid-Brown Genuine Kid Leather Lace Oxford. Genuine Goodyear Welt construction, made on a special foot-support last, with riveted steel-shank. Best oak leather outersole, grain leather innersole and rubber capped heel.

Styles for all occasions, genuine Goodyear welt, great for golfing and hiking. Blucher oxfords, Palm Beach canvas, patent, calfskin, or tan calf-finish models, fabulous for foot support and a handsome look.

Newest Spring Model
Genuine Goodyear Welts at $3.49

The "Ritz"

7 H C2441 Men's
Patent Leather
Sizes: 5½ to 11.
$3.49
Postage, 12c Extra

Men's Patent Leather Lace Oxford, with the new, cleverly designed embossing on the quarter giving the shoe an unusually attractive and snappy appearance. Good quality Patent Leather uppers, grain leather innersole, light weight, close-trimmed leather outersole, rubber capped heel and neat, dressy medium plain toe last. Genuine Goodyear Welt.

This nobby Blucher Oxford made on a medium-high round toe last, with high military heel, is of Tan Calf-finished Leather, neatly perforated on tip and quarter, and with a scalloped tip effect giving the shoe an unusually neat appearance. Brass eyelets and two rows of Goodyear stitching; both features are very prominent this season. Genuine Goodyear Welt.

Newest Sport Model

7 H C2434 Men's—Black
7 H C2435 Men's—Tan
Sizes: 5½ to 11.
$3.49
Postage, 12c Extra

Your choice of either Tan or Black in this new, smart Blucher Oxford with stylish design embossed on tip and quarter. This embossing is the newest style feature of the season and is in strong demand by particular dressers. Built on medium, semi-balloon toe last, with grain leather innersole, oak leather outersole, and springy rubber heel. Genuine Goodyear Welt.

For Young Men of Fashion

7 H C2433 Men's—Tan
Sizes: 5½ to 11.
$3.49
Postage, 12c Extra

Blucher Oxford of Tan Calf-finish Leather, printed in the new alligator effect. Three-point tip, vamp and quarter stitched with harness thread. Heel has rolled edge and rubber cap. Grain leather innersole, oak leather outersole; Genuine Goodyear Welt construction.

Double Goodyear Stitching

7 H C2439 Men's—Tan
Sizes: 5½ to 11.
$3.49
Postage, 12c Extra

The Featherweight

A Classy Black Oxford

7 H C2432 Men's—Tan
Sizes: 5½ to 11.
$3.49
Postage, 12c Extra

Smart Blucher Oxford of Black Calf-finished Leather. With contrasting gray harness stitching. Oblong nickel eyelets. Rubber capped heel has rolled edge. Oak leather outersole; medium semi-balloon toe last.

For Outdoor Sports

Men's High Shoes		$3.49
7 H C2100	Black	
7 H C2123	Tan	
Men's Oxford		Sizes:
7 H C2600	Black	5½ to 11.
7 H C2601	Tan	Postage, 12c Extra

Your choice of either high or low cut, Black or Tan Calf-finished Leather in this popular featherweight model. Neatly stitched on tip, vamp and quarter. Has small pin-hole perforations and midget eyelets that add to its dignity. Made over a medium round

7 H C2431 Men's—Tan
Sizes: 5½ to 11.
Tan Calf-finish
$3.49
Postage, 12c Extra

Comfort and Style

7 H C2436 Men's—Black
Sizes: 5½ to 11.
$3.49
Postage, 12c Extra

For young men of fashion. Patent leather lace oxfords, nobby Blucher oxford with scalloped tip, classic Blucher oxfords in alligator effect. Featherweight black or tan calf-finished tall or short shoes, neatly stitched on vamp. All with genuine Goodyear welt.

120

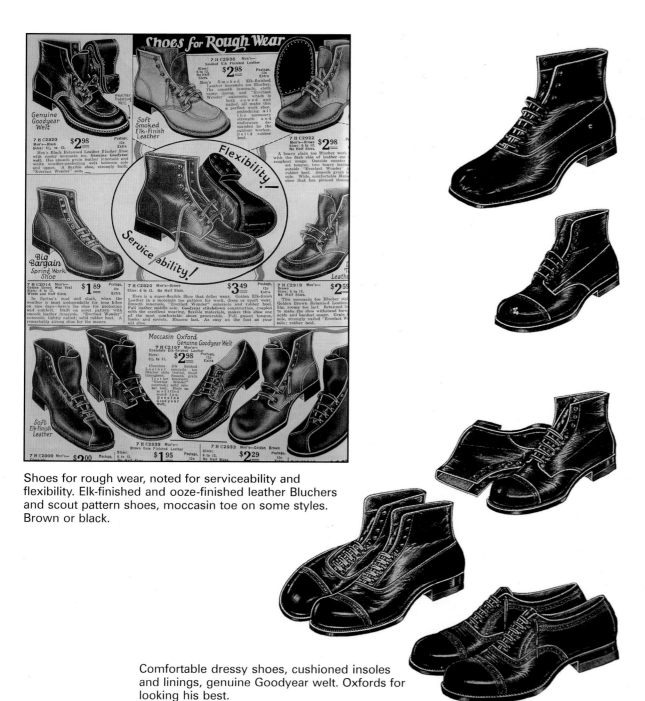

Shoes for rough wear, noted for serviceability and flexibility. Elk-finished and ooze-finished leather Bluchers and scout pattern shoes, moccasin toe on some styles. Brown or black.

Comfortable dressy shoes, cushioned insoles and linings, genuine Goodyear welt. Oxfords for looking his best.

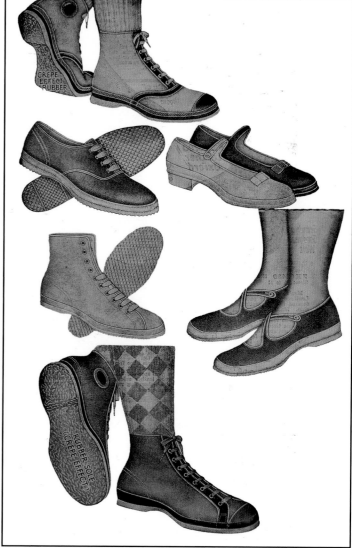

For the sportsman in us all... canvas athletic shoes and sandals for men, boys, and children. Brown and white.

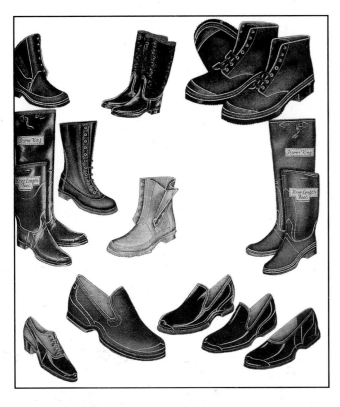

Brown canvas work shoes for men and boys, sportsmen's special for rough wear. Sturdy boots that give protection from rain and slush for the entire family, including women's foothold that fits any shoe. Storm rubbers or military and cow heeled rubber mocs for women.

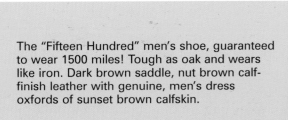

Strong, dressy shoes for real boys, genuine Goodyear welts.

The "Fifteen Hundred" men's shoe, guaranteed to wear 1500 miles! Tough as oak and wears like iron. Dark brown saddle, nut brown calf-finish leather with genuine, men's dress oxfords of sunset brown calfskin.

Men's stout wearing scout style shoes of elk leather, work Bluchers of waxed veal leather, black vici kid, calf finish leather sport oxfords, and white Nu-Buck sport oxfords, with brown calf skin trim. Strong, sturdy rubber soles and Goodyear welts.

Stylish hats for gents, fur felt, serge, linen, or suitings, in the highest styles and fashions. The "Carlsbad" style with slightly curled brim and grosgrain band and bow is *the* hat to have for spring. Lightweight golf caps and sennit straw also a good pick for the warmer weather.

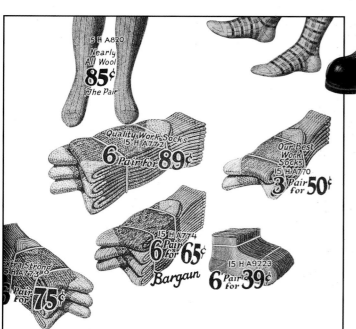

Dependable socks for every man. All wool sports hose, quality work socks. Thick, heavy-weight cotton for support and warmth. Striped, patterned, and solids with double heels and toes.

Genuine fur felt hat with plain edge, convertible brim, fancy silk grosgrain band, swagger style for dress or sports wear. Carlsbad style with soft, silky sheen… holds shape despite the weather.

Stylish hats and caps worn by smart New York men. Genuine Panama, "stadium" wool felt hat, tan straw hat with rough fancy weave, smart golf and polo caps, collegiate, Broadway fur felt, and "congress" fur felt styles. A look to suit any gentleman. Tan, brown, steel gray, black.

Wool felt crusher hat, black, gray, and brown, and sport visor for outdoor sport or work, green celluloid eyeshield. Pieced top style cap with popular circular plaid effect, gray plaid, tan plaid, powder blue.

Men's nightwear and bathrobes, made full and roomy. Cotton pongee, genuine broadcloth, amply long pants. Fruit of the loom nightgown, round cut-away neck, double yoke, breast pocket. Terrycloth robe, ideal for home comfort, for the beach, or bath, novelty cord edges and belt.

Two tone blazer striped pajamas, soft finish cotton pongee, long full cut pants. Men's nightgown of white muslin, round cutaway neck, roomy and comfortable.

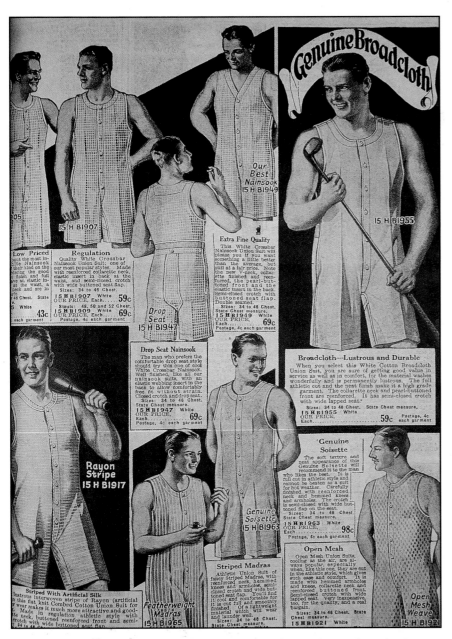

Genuine broadcloth union suits for him, nainsook crossbar styles, elastic webbing for flexibility and comfort.

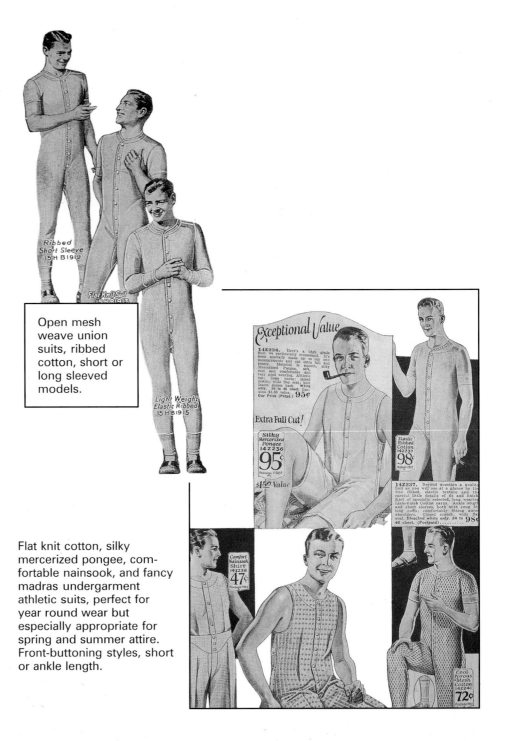

Open mesh weave union suits, ribbed cotton, short or long sleeved models.

Flat knit cotton, silky mercerized pongee, comfortable nainsook, and fancy madras undergarment athletic suits, perfect for year round wear but especially appropriate for spring and summer attire. Front-buttoning styles, short or ankle length.

Children Fashions

Charming Clothes for Young Girls

Charming, summery dresses, and stunning new coats and capes for young beauties. Colorful and distinctive, with frills, ruffles, belts, buckles, and buttons to make each dress unique and pretty!

Bright and sassy, young girls are sure to shine in rich, colorful frocks of voile, linene, batiste, rayon, charmeuse, broadcloth, and gingham.

Smart frocks featuring Peter Pan collars, embroidered appliqués, picoted ruffles, and ribbon and silk bows to complete the look.

Ideal dresses of white organdy, flowered rayon, woven check tissue gingham, or ruffled voile for summer fun.

Cotton Peter Pan, linene polka dots, figured rayon, and Kalburnie chambray dresses in sharp, bright summer colors.

Dresses perfect for school wear or play, novelty prints, smart styles.

2^{98}

4^{98}

2^{49}

62

"FadeNot"
Linene
34Z951
1^{98}
POST-FREE

"FadeNot"
Linene
34Z950
1^{89}
POST-FREE

Mercerized
Pongee
34Z953
1^{98}
POST-FREE

Linene
34Z952
1^{49}
POST-FREE

Party dress of beautiful all silk crepe de Chine with picoted ruffles and corded flower waistline, all silk pongee dress with hand embroidered front and pocket, and novelty tussah one-piece frock with silk ribbon.

Frocks of fast color linene, mercerized pongee, with decorative hand embroidery, skirts with box and side pleats, novel shaped pockets, sashes, and bows.

Plaid or solid color gingham, appliqué dotted voile, khaki service cloth, and linene sport suits and dresses, great for fun in the summer sun.

Hand Emb'd. Rajah
34 Z 961
$1.98
POST. FREE

Hand Emb'd. Voile
34 Z 960
$1.98
POST. FREE

3 Piece Suit Silk Finished Rajah
34 Z 963
$2.98
POST. FREE

Hand Emb'd. Voile
34 Z 962
$2.79
POST. FREE

Lonsdale Jean
34 Z 964
$1.98
POST. FREE

Solid Color Gingham

Hand embroidered voile, rajah, silk finished rajah, Lonsdale jean dresses and two-piece middy suits… perfect for fashionable schoolyard dress, or weekend wear. Tan, white, tangerine, powder blue, orchid, Copenhagen blue.

Co-ed style middy of Lonsdale jean with braid-trimmed sailor collar and cuffs. Knife plaited wool crepe skirt, attached to white cambric waist. Practical khaki jean shirt, loop for tie at neck, breast pocket. Gray cotton tweed or khaki service cloth knickers, finished with buckle. Practical knickers for the athletic girl, all wool tweed.

Mercerized tan cotton pongee forms a co-ed style blouse with Peter Pan collar, pocket embroidered with tennis racket design. Blouse finished at neck with bow of silk braid. Skirt of all wool plaid tweed flannel, box plaited all around, attached to waist of good quality white cambric, blue or brown plaids.

Middy and co-ed blouses, pleated gym bloomers, and girls' knickers for sport and play, or a plaid all wool lumberjack coat for fashionable outerwear.

98¢

School girls look sassy in cambric, khaki cloth, soft suede cloth, and Lonsdale jean garments for play, or attractive school outfits.

Skirt 24 H 5688

$1.69

The schoolgirl's wardrobe needs windbreakers, shawls, and sweaters to keep her up-to-date and stylish. Fine quality wool worsted in bright, summery colors.

All Wool Worsted Honeycomb Shawls

For Mother or Babe

Special $3.98

Wool and Rayon Slip-Over $1.98

$1.79 Size 48x44 $1.98 Size 64x54

All Wool Worsted With Rayon Design

For changeable weather these All Wool Worsted Honeycomb Shawls are handy and protective, especially if there's a baby in the house to be guarded from drafts. They are attractively made with a neat woven border and fringe.
Size, about 64x54 inches including fringe.
22 H 7621 White, Black or Gray. State Color.
OUR PRICE, Each.... $1.98 Postage, 4c Extra
Same quality as above, but size about 48x44 ins. including fringe.
22 H 7620 White, Black or Gray. State Color.
OUR PRICE, Each.... $1.79 Postage, 4c Extra

Knitted Windbreakers are fashionable. This is an unusually striking model of All Wool Worsted with Rayon (artificial silk) worked in the allover pattern. Solid color pocket tops, cuffs, hip band and convertible collar. An exceptional garment at the price.
Sizes: 34 to 44. Order sweater 2 ins. larger than actual bust measure.
22 H 7124 Buff
22 H 7125 Poudre
22 H 7126 Silver
PRICE, Each.... $3.98 Postage, 8c Extra

Smart Wool Slipover featuring the student collar with a buttoned vestee of Rayon (artificial silk) while Wool makes the border of the sleeves and bottom.
Complete your costume with this up-to-the-minute model to wear with your sport skirt.
Sizes: 34 to 44. Order sweater 2 inches larger than actual bust measure.
22 H 7021 Poudre Blue
22 H 7022 Buff
22 H 7023 Wine
PRICE, Each.... $1.98 Postage, 8c Extra

Misses' All Wool Shaker Knit Coat $4.65

Sizes 34 to 38 For 14 to 18 Years

Knit-in Pockets

The High School and college girls' choice for general sports wear is this rugged Shaker Knit Coat Sweater of All Wool. It is good looking and made to give years of service. The big, 5-piece double knit shawl collar may be buttoned up high. Collar, pockets and sleeves are all knit in, so are much stronger than if only sewed on.
Sizes: 34 to 38. For Ages 14 to 18 years. Order sweater 2 inches larger than actual Bust measure. State Age and Sweater Size.

Sizes 28 to 36 For Girls 6 to 14 Years

Girls' All Wool Worsted Wind-Breaker $2.98

To be up-to-date, the school girl's wardrobe needs a trig Windbreaker like this one of All Wool Worsted. A fancy allover diamond pattern covers the body and sleeves; the collar, cuffs, hip band and the buttoned flaps of the two pockets are in solid color. Collar may be worn as illustrated or buttoned up in semi-student style.
Sizes: 28 to 36. For ages 6 to 14 years. Order sweater 2 inches larger than actual Bust measure. State Age and Sweater Size.
22 H 7961 Poudre Blue
22 H 7963 Jockey Red
22 H 7965 Buff
PRICE, Each.... $2.98 Postage, 8c Extra

Brushed Sport Wool

The unusually fine texture, so close as almost to resemble cloth, makes this elastic ribbed knit All Wool Worsted Sports Coat splendidly warm and yet light in weight. Smart New York women favor it for every sports occasion. Decidedly new style touches are the deep border of contrasting knitting on the pockets and hem and the V-neck collar, which when buttoned up becomes the popular student style. All seams are strong and beautifully finished.
Sizes: 36 to 46. Order sweater 2 inches larger than actual Bust measure. State Size.
22 H 7073 Gendarme Blue
22 H 7074 Buff
22 H 7075 Cocoa Brown
PRICE, Each.... $4.69 Postage, 10c Extra

All Wool Worsted Elastic Ribbed Knit Sport Coat $4.69

All wool tweed flannel knickers, perfect for sports. Or three-piece tan khaki or gray mixture cotton tweed sport suit, sleeveless jacket, knickers, and blouse of mercerized cotton pongee, trimmed at the neck with a small black bow.

Three-Piece
Khaki
Sport Suit
34Z940
$2⁹⁸
POSTAGE
FREE

All Wool
Tweed
Flannel
34Z941
$2⁹⁸
Postage
FREE

Right:
Splendidly tailored, thick and warm coats for inclement months ahead. Tan, brick (the new reddish shade), ashes of roses, Arab.

All Wool
Blocked
Polaire
48Z833
$7⁹⁸
POST.
FREE

All Wool
Polaire
Full Lined
48Z831
$7⁹⁸
POST.
FREE

All Wool
Kashmir
Polaire
48Z834
$10⁹⁸
POST.
FREE

All Wool
Plaid
Polaire
48Z830
$2⁹⁸
POST.
FREE

All Wool
Polaire
Full Lined
48Z824
$6 98 POST. FREE

All Wool
Blocked
Polaire
Full Lined
48Z821
$8 49 POST. FREE

Beautiful coats of all wool blocked polaire, fully lined, with two or four novelty button closures.

Girls Dainty Muslin Underwear and Night Wear!

All Postage FREE!

Satin Striped Radium 26Z400 26Z401 **98¢** UP POST FREE

26Z402 26Z403 **98¢** POST FREE

26Z404 **79¢** POST FREE

Pincheck Nainsook 26Z405 **79¢** POST FREE

Pincheck Nainsook 26Z405 **79¢** POST FREE

Woven Crepe 26Z406 26Z407 **98¢** UP POST FREE

Girls' dainty muslin underwear and nightwear. All silk princess slips of lustrous satin stripe radium, or fine white longcloth. White cambric or checked nainsook longie pajamas, front closing with silk frogs, flesh or white. Blue bird patterned woven crepe pajamas, shirring at front.

Dainty Styles for Girls

Dainty styles for girls, slips, nightgowns, and two piece pajama sets with long pants, white and flesh.

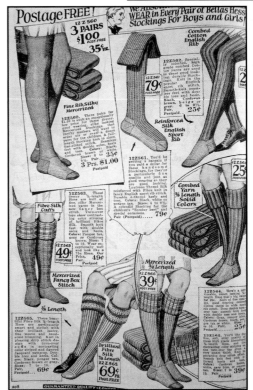

Postage FREE!

We ALSO WEAR in Every Pair of Bettas Hess Stockings For Boys and Girls!

Stockings for boys and girls, fine rib silky mercerized, combed cotton English rib, combed yarn models. White, gray, brown.

Smart Fashions for Smart Boys

Smart suits for smart boys… just like Dad's, but smaller! Made of all wool tweed, worsted, serge, cassimere, in every style for any type of young man!

Fashionably tailored high school suits, in a variety of weaves. All wool styles in glen plaid cheviot, fine weave serge, three-color striped cassimere, many with extra trousers.

Beautifully tailored suits for youths of high school and college age. All wool cassimere or tweed, shapely trousers and attractive lines, snappy, serviceable, and comfortable. Lined with excellent quality all wool alpaca. Horizon blue, medium brown, dark blue serge.

Stylish striped wool cassimere suit, trousers with plain or cuff bottoms. Brown or blue-gray. Youth's overall suit made of heavy weight, staunchly woven serviceable khaki drill with triple stitched seams for wear and tear. Neat, well tailored trousers for dress, sport, or everyday wear of all wool tweed in brown or gray.

Be just like dad! Fancy patterned all wool slip-over and coat-style sweaters, swagger style, colorful and vivid for summer wear.

138

Boys' wearproof suits, two-or three-button single breasted coats, longies or matching knickers, in the latest styles to mimic dad.

Excellent quality wool suits for boys, longies or knickers, in fine twilled cheviot, or all wool worsted.

All wool guaranteed suits, overplaid cheviot, fine twilled cheviot, or diagonal cheviot. Fully lined knickers, extra separate longies.

Extra "Longies"
4 H B712
$1.98

Extra "Longies"
4 H B887
$1.79

Extra "Longies"
4 H B716
$1.98

All Wool
Cheviot
Three Piece
Suit
4 H B714
$6.98

Latest
Weave
4 H B710
$8.49

All Wool
Tweed Suit
with
Golf Knickers
4 H B885
$4.98

Handsome, double breasted suit, wide peak lapel, longies with cuff bottoms. All wool twilled cheviot or all wool tweed suits, complete outfits of knickers, coat, and slip-over sweater, extra mannish style longies. All wool glen plaid cheviot suit, two button English style with vest.

4 H B601
$1.98

Cassimere
or Serge
4 H B611
$2.79

All Wool
Tweed or
All Wool
Cheviot
4 H B696
$3.79

"Longie"
Suit
4 H B664
$3.79

All Wool
Over Plaid
Cheviot
4 H B678
$5.98

Extra
Longies
4 H B670
$1.39

Durable
Serge
Two Piece
Knicker Suit
4 H B669
$3.89

Two Piece
"Longie" Suit
4 H B674
$3.98

All Wool
Tweed
4 H B660
$4.98

Little fellows' sailor outfits, longie and shortie suits, and dressy coats. Made of durable wools, rayons, serge. All pants in straight style, becoming to little ones.

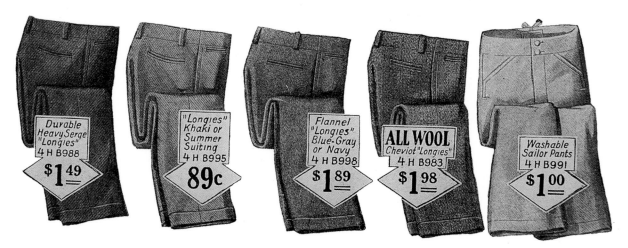

Long wearing heavy weight serge, khaki summer suiting, fine quality flannel, all wool cheviot, and washable white sailor pants, strongly sewn in regulation men's style but for the young gent. Straight, wide bottoms with a cuff.

Boys' and young mens' comfortable summer sports blouses of good quality khaki, colored shirting, or color stripe percale feature sport collar, elbow length sleeves, and breast pocket.

Every boy, big or little, likes sailor longies! Heavy wool mixed flannel, staunchly tailored, buttons in front, laced back, wide straight bottoms, with a watch pocket. Navy blue, gray.

Regulation Sailor Pants of Heavy Excellent Quality Navy Blue Flannel 4 H B986 $1.98

Boys' khaki and denim workwear, moleskin or corduroy breeches.

Refinement and good taste in these attractively striped flannel, all wool cassimere, and navy serge students and collegian trousers. Blue gray, medium gray, and dark navy blue.

Heavy weight double and twist indigo blue denim workwear, securely reinforced and bartacked. Work jacket has three deep pockets and rust proof riveted buttons. Overalls have double thickness in front and at knees, with four pockets each.

Novelty Suit

Wool
Cassimere
9Z821
$3 85
POST. FREE

With 2
Pair of
Knickers

All Wool
Worsted
Serge
9Z823
$5 98

All Wool
9Z838
$6 98
POST. FREE

EXTRA
KNICKERS

All Wool
Cassimere
With 2 Pair
of Knickers
9Z837
$7 98
POST FREE

CAP
9Z868

Wool
Cassimere
9Z835
$3 98
With 2 Pair
of Full Lined
Knickers
9Z836
$4 98
POST.FREE

All Wool
Worsted
Serge
9Z842
$7 48
POST. FREE

EXTRA
KNICKERS

Stoutly built clothes for the little fellow! Oliver Twist and novelty suits, stylish knickers and trousers in the best materials – all wool cassimere, twill, all wool jersey, and twill serge.

With 2 Pairs of Knickers 9Z850 $6.98 POSTAGE FREE

Nobby All Wool Tweed Suit

EXTRA KNICKERS

EXTRA GOLF KNICKERS

9Z852 Smart All Wool Cassimere 2 Pairs of Knickers $9.65 POSTAGE FREE

All wool tweed suit, fully lined knickers and smartly cut, full lined single breasted Norfolk coat with yoke and inverted plaits in back, gray, or brown. Snappy sport suit with regular and golf-style knickers, made of all wool cassimere with neat, subdued over-plaids in either medium brown or blue-gray.

Suits for boys modeled after the heroes of war. French and Balkan sailor suits, middy suits, and Oliver Twist styles in blues, khaki greens, tans, and grays.

Dressy Little Wash Suits
All Modestly Priced and Postage FREE!

IMPORTED ENGLISH BROADCLOTH

EXTRA PANTS

Pure Linen

New Three-Piece Novelty Suit

Tan Cotton Pongee With Sport Belt

Washable Miami Linen with Two Pairs of Pants

Three Piece Sport Play Suit

Pure Linen 9Z927 $1.95 POST FREE

Extra Peggy Cloth Pants

High Grade White Jean

Smart, sturdy, and good looking wash suits for active boys. Two- and three-piece playsuits decorated with silk braiding on collar or front button-through pockets. Brown, blue, jasper.

144

Tan cotton pongee, Lonsdale jean, and domestic broadcloth serviceable suits for little boys, sturdy and durable for play.

Serviceable tan khaki drill double seat laced breeches, bartacked at all points of strain. Durable double seat corduroy laced breeches, wear-resisting drab velveteen, securely reinforced at points of strain.

Pure linen suits, coat with yoke and knife plaits front and back, full roomy stitched knickers or straight short pants. Baseball outfit of gray flannel, double stitched shirt, bloomer pants with back pocket. Sport camp outfit, turned down stockings of combed cotton, roomy laced breeches and scout hat to complete the look, durable khaki drill. Eight piece cowboy playsuit, blouse, long pants, hat, pistol, belt, holster, lariat, bandana handkerchief. Three piece Indian play outfit, washable khaki drill, blouse, and long pants with fancy trimming and bonnet with gay feathers.

Sturdy overalls and playsuits for boys, khaki jean, indigo blue denim, or khaki drill weight garments for hard work or play. Reinforced double stitching all over, sporty shirts and long or short pants.

Rip Proof

Khaki Drill Overall Suit 9Z955 $1.00 POST FREE

Good Weight Indigo Blue Denim 9Z959 9Z960 79¢ UP POST FREE

BAR TACKS

Khaki Drill or Staunch Blue Overall Suiting 9Z961 9Z962 59¢ UP POST FREE

Boys' Complete Khaki Outdoor Outfit 4 H B556

Traffic Cop Outfit 4 H B551 $2.69

Smart Combination Lumber Jack Suit 4 H B615

Cowboy Outfit in Two Grades 4 H B506 $1.48

4 H B517 98c

Young lads love to pretend! Like a boy scout, traffic cop, lumberjack, or cowboy, these playsuits come with all the real accessories that any young dreamer would love to have!

146

Men's and Boy's nightshirts and pajamas, made of fine mercerized pongee and soft but durable pajama cloth. Each ornamented with silk frogs or fancy trimming braid and buttons. Blue, white, tan.

No Buttons

Buttonless pajamas, soft finish cotton pongee, trimmed with contrasting color, breast pocket, and select models finished with silk frogs, white, tan, and blue.

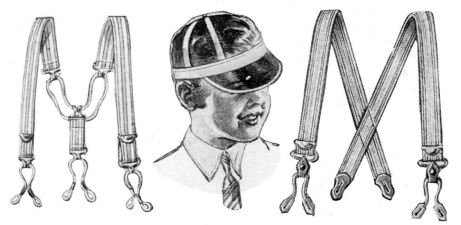

Every boy needs at least one... or two! Suspenders for dress and play. 32 inches long, sliding adjustable metal buttons, in an assortment of neat mannish colors. Sport visor for outdoor play protects the eyes from sun.

Fashions for Infants and Tiny Tots

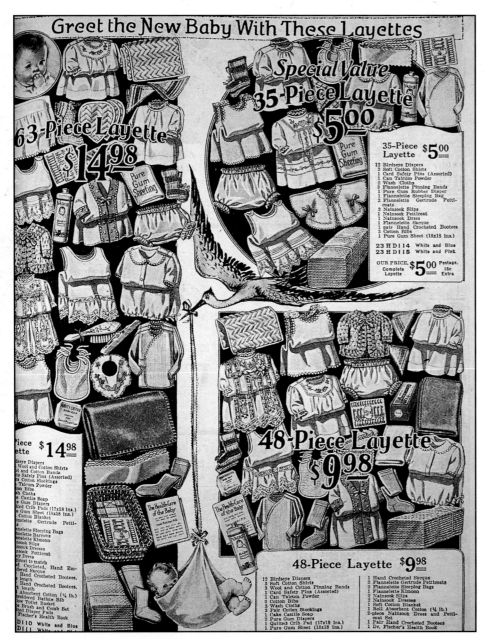

Greet the New Baby With These Layettes

Special Value
35-Piece Layette
$5.00
Pure Gum Sheeting

63-Piece Layette
$14.98
Pure Gum Sheeting

35-Piece $5.00 Layette

12 Birdseye Diapers
2 Soft Cotton Shirts
1 Card Safety Pins (Assorted)
1 Can Talcum Powder
2 Wash Cloths
3 Flannelette Pinning Bands
1 Pure Gum Rubber Diaper
1 Flannelette Sleeping Bag
2 Flannelette Gertrude Petticoats
2 Nainsook Slips
1 Nainsook Petticoat
1 Nainsook Dress
1 Flannelette Sacque
1 pair Hand Crocheted Bootees
3 Cotton Bibs
1 Pure Gum Sheet (18x18 ins.)

23 HD 114 White and Blue
23 HD 115 White and Pink

OUR PRICE,
Complete
Layette **$5.00**
Postage,
18c
Extra

48-Piece Layette
$9.98

Piece ette $14.98

seye Diapers
Wool and Cotton Shirts
and Cotton Bands
ds Safety Pins (Assorted)
s Cotton Stockings
Talcum Powder
on Bibs
sh Cloths
e Castile Soap
e Gum Diapers
ted Crib Pads (17x18 ins.)
e Gum Sheet (18x18 ins.)
Cotton Blanket
nelette Gertrude Petti-
nelette Sleeping Bags
nelette Barrows
nelette Kimono
nsook Slips
nsook Dresses
Petticoat
coat to match
Crocheted, Hand Em-
ered Sacque
Hand Crocheted Bootees,
length
Hand Crocheted Bootees,
length
Absorbent Cotton (¼ lb.)
broidered Battiste Bib
ow Toilet Basket
Brush and Comb Set
ted Diaper Pads
Fischer's Health Book

D110 White and Blue
D111 White an

48-Piece Layette $9.98

12 Birdseye Diapers
3 Soft Cotton Shirts
3 Wool and Cotton Pinning Bands
1 Card Safety Pins (Assorted)
1 Can Talcum Powder
3 Cotton Bibs
2 Wash Cloths
1 Pair Cotton Stockings
1 Cake Castile Soap
2 Pure Gum Diapers
1 Quilted Crib Pad (17x18 ins.)
1 Pure Gum Sheet (18x18 ins.)

1 Hand Crocheted Sacque
2 Flannelette Gertrude Petticoats
2 Flannelette Sleeping Bags
1 Flannelette Kimono
2 Nainsook Slips
2 Nainsook Dresses
1 Soft Cotton Blanket
1 Roll Absorbent Cotton (¼ lb.)
2-piece Nainsook Dress and Petticoat Set
1 Pair Hand Crocheted Bootees
1 Dr. Fischer's Health Book

C.W.S. Tie Wrapper
No Pins

Choice 15¢ Each

Rayon-Wool and Cotton 39¢

23 H D811   23 H D812

Cotton Knitted 35¢

Choice of Materials 23¢ Up

Summer comforts for baby – shirts and wrappers of combed cotton, cotton diaper drawers or band shirts of wool, cotton, and rayon, combining warmth, durability, and a smooth surface.

Greet the new baby with these layettes! Everything you need to get started with your little one! Diapers, bibs, washcloths, crib pads, blankets, and more. 35-piece, 48- piece, or 63- piece sets, in white and blue or white and pink.

Batiste
23 H D785
59¢

23 H D784
39¢

23 H D781
49¢

Nainsook
23 H D786
3 for 50¢

23 H D782
49¢

White Nainsook and cambric underclothes and nightgowns for little ones.

3-Piece Set   Wool
All Wool   3-Piece Set

$1⁴⁹

Hand Embroide
$1⁹⁸

nd oidered
85¢

Ray
98

79¢

Bargain

All wool hand embroidered sweaters, pure worsted, flannel lumberjack styles. Navy, red, peacock, assorted plaids and stripes.

Pretty frocks, rompers, and boy's suits for little girls. Summery fabrics in loose, breezy styles and the brightest, sweetest colors.

Coats, dresses, and even hats for the big sister… always the little lady. Voile, mercerized cotton pongee, rajah cloth, chambray, and other smart, strong fabrics make up these dainty dresses and delightful coats and capes.

Middy suits and dainty dresses for thrifty mothers who want to dress the little ones well. In solids and prints, khaki jean, blue peggy cloth, or assorted colors.

Color-splashed dresses and playsuits for summer fun.

Little girls' styles mock their mothers, in delicate and colorful hats and outerwear. Reds, pinks, and blues, all getting them ready for the blustery months ahead.

Keep them warm with wool-mixed and cotton cashmere coats, robes, and wraps. Pink, blue, or white.

Your little one will look sweeter than ever in these winsome dresses, all made with attractive embroidery accents, yokes, scallops, and cluster tucks. Pink, blue, peach, white.

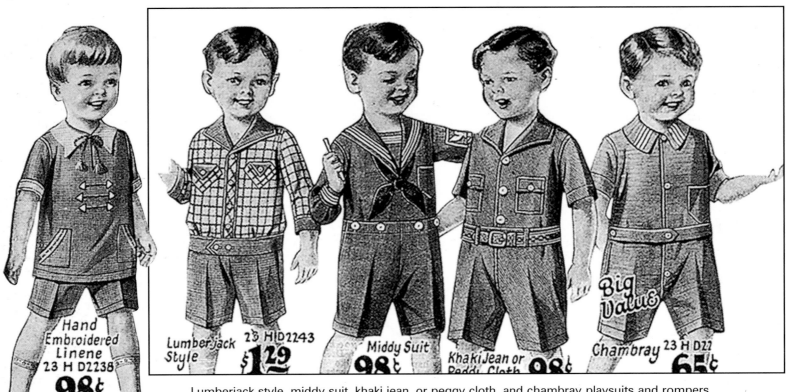

Hand
Embroidered
Linene
23 H D2238
98¢

Lumberjack
Style
23 H D2243
$1.29

Middy Suit
98¢

Khaki Jean or
Peddi Cloth
98¢

Big
Value
Chambray
23 H D22
65¢

Lumberjack style, middy suit, khaki jean, or peggy cloth, and chambray playsuits and rompers for little boys. Blue, tan, honeydew, green, khaki.

Nainsook, crossbar, cotton pongee, washenrede crepe, and cambric pajamas with drop seat.
Solids and patterns.

Children will enjoy these cool garments, elastic ribbed white cotton waist union suits, button front styles, for girls, fitted knee or umbrella knee.

Elastic Knit Waist Suit
15 H B1109
39¢ Each

15 H B1147
38¢ Each Suit

15 H B1143

15 H B1207
3 For 29¢

Hand made and hand embroidered voile and linene dresses,
cadet blue, tangerine, white, flesh pink, powder blue, maize.

Cap
41Z222

41Z243
$2⁷⁹
POST. FREE

All Wool
Crepe
41Z240
$3⁴⁹
POST. FREE

All Wool
Serge
41Z241
$2⁹⁸
POST. FREE

All Silk
Crepe
de Chine
41Z242
$3⁴⁹
POST. FREE

41Z245
$1⁹⁸
POST. FREE

Coats and capes for infants and tiny tots! All wool crepe
with delicate hand embroidery, all silk crepe de Chine,
lined and interlined. All wool serge coat, collar trimmed
with white silk and embroidery, silk braid finishes the
collar. Long white infants' coat of creame white wool-
mixed cashmere, embroidery and silk scalloping for effect.

Pretty and practical, coats of cream white wool-mix cashmere, for the tiniest of little ladies. Hand embroidered, silk scalloping, all with caps to match.

41Z249
$1⁹⁸
POST FREE

Wool Crepe
41Z250
$2⁵⁹
POST FREE

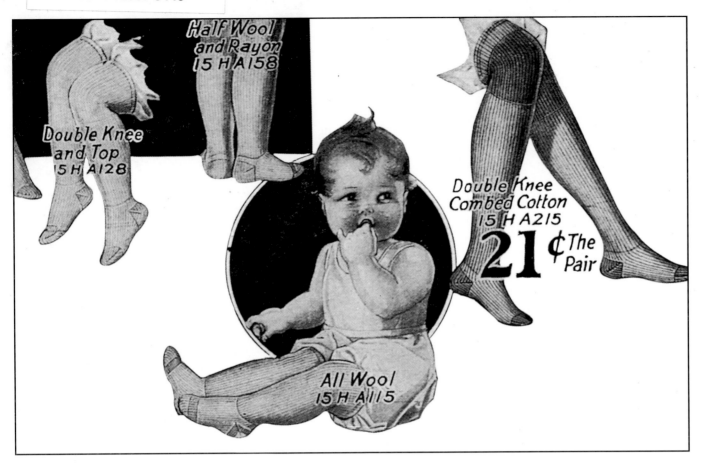

Half Wool
and Rayon
15 H A 158

Double Knee
and Top
15 H A 128

Double Knee
Combed Cotton
15 H A 215
21¢ The
Pair

All Wool
15 H A 115

Comfort for little feet. Cotton and mercerized Lisle stockings, cashmere wool, double knee and toe, thick and warm to protect. Black, white, brown, pink, blue.

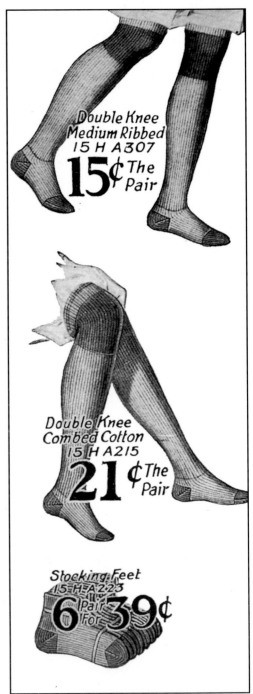

Double Knee
Medium Ribbed
15 H A 307
15¢ The
Pair

Double Knee
Combed Cotton
15 H A 215
21¢ The
Pair

Stocking Feet
15 H A 223
6 Pair
For **39¢**